IN HIM THE FULLNESS

IN HIM
THE FULLNESS

Homiletic Studies in Paul's
Epistle to the Colossians

R. E. O. WHITE

FLEMING H. REVELL COMPANY
OLD TAPPAN, NEW JERSEY

Library of Congress Cataloging in Publication Data

White, Reginald E   0
   In Him the fullness.

   1. Bible. N. T. Colossians—Sermons.
2. Baptists—Sermons. 3. Sermons, English.
I. Title.
BS2715.4.W5   227'.7'066   73–8801
ISBN 0–8007–0620–X

Contents

Introduction

These expository meditations focus upon
the cosmic significance of Christ and the
consequent depth, breadth, and height of
Christian experience.

Like the Epistle to the Colossians upon
which they are based, they have special
relevance for Christians facing the limitless
horizons of an ever-expanding universe,
and the ever-increasing complexity of
Christian discipleship.

Their theme is Paul's theme: the inexhaustible
sufficiency of Jesus Christ our Lord, in
all the situations in which Christians
find themselves, in any age.

—R. E. O. WHITE

Christ in Colossians

1

The Christ, the Christian, and the Church
COLOSSIANS 1:1-5a

"Christianity is ikons, pictures, good-for-nothing monks, ignorant priests doing altar magic to impress the superstitious. Christianity is nothing to do with *that* (pushing away a New Testament). It is teaching peasants to keep their place, manipulating government in the interest of the privileged; it is blessing war, and resisting revolution."

On a hillside above Sian, in China, two men discussed what had brought them there together—one, a Christian missionary from northern England, the other a Communist commandant, trained in Moscow. The missionary told his life story, shaped by the teaching of the New Testament, crystallizing in a call to service and evangelism in distant China in obedience to Christ. That testimony had provoked the above protest—a protest based, naturally, on the only version of Christianity which the Communist had ever known.

Explanation took a long time. There, overlooking one of the oldest cities in the world, two dedicated men discussed one of the oldest topics in the world, religion, and the inescapable question, asked a thousand times by friend and foe alike—what *is* Christianity?

That question is almost unanswerable because the subject is almost indefinable and the full meaning inexhaustible. Slick slogans merely obscure the richness of the truth. "Christianity is Christ," say some, truly enough, but leaving so much unexplained. "Christianity is salvation—the heart's experience of God," others would say, again truly enough, but leaving so much out. "Christianity is commitment—loyal adherence to the church and all her sacred standards," say yet others, taking a great deal for granted. In the end, we may be better served by seeing Christianity in operation, watching what it does and how it does it, and leaving definitions to those who like to theorize.

That Christ, the Christian experience, and the life and work of the church lie close together in such inquiries is obvious. Because in his letter to the Colossians Paul is defending the essence of Christianity

11

from misrepresentation, he begins by setting Christ, the Christian, and the church in clear relationship. To explain Christianity, we must understand the absolute centrality of Christ, the nature of the Christian experience, and the significance of the church.

The Centrality of Christ

The name of Christ stands in the opening verses like the key signature to some great symphony. Four times (if not five) Jesus is named, either as "Jesus Christ"—the Man born to be King, or as "Christ Jesus"—the Man now risen and exalted. Deliberately and skillfully Paul sets the theme of all that is to follow.

For Christ is the subject of Colossians, Christ in His universal splendor, Christ in His cosmic significance and inexhaustible fullness. The Christian with his problems, and the church with its responsibilities, are also in Paul's mind: but both are seen in the light of Christ, who alone can make a man a Christian, and set the Christian within His church. Indeed, everything in this letter is focused upon Christ; everything in Christian faith and activity is made to depend upon our comprehension of His greatness, our experience of His fullness.

(1) It is through Christ that God the Father is made known. Certainly other times have known something of God, and other peoples. He has not left himself without a witness in any age or land. Paul, too, had known God in some fashion long before he met Christ. But henceforth Christ is the clue to all that God is—"God, the Father of our Lord, Jesus Christ." Though no man has seen God at any time, the Son has declared Him. John warns bluntly: he that has the Son has the Father also, but he that has not the Son has not the Father. So the Master Himself had said: no man knows the Son save the Father, and no man knows the Father save the Son, and he to whom the Son will reveal Him. Paul strikes this essential note at once. All the highest that we know of God, of His deity and fatherhood, of His power and love, and of His purposes, we owe to Christ, through whom the Father is made known.

(2) In Christ the Christian's faith is focused. As Jesus defines God, so He defines also the Christian's faith. It is faith *in* or resting upon Christ Jesus. We do not live by some vague confidence in the ultimate goodness of things but by vital commitment to trust in Christ Himself. Without Christ, faith reaches empty hands to unresponsive air,

and grasps at dreams; in Him faith finds its anchorage, its confirmation, and its exceeding great reward.

(3) In Christ the Christian life is lived. The saints and faithful brethren are themselves "in Christ Jesus," living in two environments, *in Colossae* and *in Christ.* As the physical environment exerts its pressure on a man, makes its demands, shapes his days, so the inner, psychological and spiritual environment, our being *in Christ,* exerts pressures and offers resource. That was the simple but basic secret of being a saint amidst paganism; the secret, too, of astonishing endurance. For whatever the pain and the peril, to be in Christ was to be at heart out of this world and beyond the reach of harm.

(4) To Christ all Christian service is rendered. Paul is "an apostle of Christ Jesus"; outside of Christ, he has no authority, no mission, no message, and no power. To make Christ fully known is his life's overriding ambition. Much else needs to be done in the world, and by Christians, in caring for men and opposing wrong; but always for Christ's sake. The driving motive that sustains all Christian activity never descends to sentimental humanitarianism, nor to the relief of a bad conscience about society. Christian service is offered to all as those for whom Christ died, and offered out of gratitude and love toward Him who first loved us.

So central is Christ to all Christian thinking about God, faith, experience, and work. This letter insists that to every problem, every perplexity, every demand and discontent, Christ is the answer—and the sufficient answer. That is what Paul writes to say. In that sense, Christ is Christianity. But Paul adds more.

The Dimensions of Christian Life

From the sufficiency of Christ, it follows that life focused upon Him must be full and sufficient; from the greatness of Christ follows the largeness of Christian experience.

Paul never uses words lightly. The gentile Christians at Colossae are *saints*—among the people of God set apart for His name. They are *brethren* welcomed into the fellowship of all who own Jesus as Lord. To add *in Christ* is to affirm the most wonderful privilege that could be afforded to any man.

But that is not all. Using a form of description which he inherited

from those in Christ before him, Paul gives thanks for the Colossians'
faith, and *love,* and *hope.* Those three qualities distinguish the Christian man. His life is built upon a deep conviction, constrained by a
warm affection, illumined by a glowing expectation. And when these
characteristics are examined, each is seen to be an enlargement of
soul, a liberating of mind and heart and spirit. Faith, love, and hope
open the prison house for them that are bound, and set men free in
the largeness of God's world and the liberty of God's love.

(1) For *faith* reaches upwards, out of life's inhibiting limitations toward God and all goodness. It refuses to be confined to earth's material and temporal boundaries, claiming its birthright in the realm of
spirit. Faith links our littleness with God's greatness, our wavering
courage with God's unwearying strength, our fearful hearts with His
almighty love, our life's little day with God's eternity. All life is larger
for those who have faith—they traffic with the infinite.

(2) By *love* the soul reaches outward to surmount its own isolation,
its mere individuality and self-centeredness, and enter the larger
world of fellowship, compassion, brotherhood. Christian love is an
endless adventure in friendship, fraught with immeasurable discoveries of the variety and goodness and interest of people. Its demands
are never fully met and its challenges constantly stretch our capaci-
ties, but its surprises never cease to delight and its rewards are beyond
price. Love certainly enlarges life.

(3) And so does *hope.* By hope, man rebels against the limitation of
his horizons and claims forever. Hope reaches forward from the
present with its frustrations and fears to a future bright with the promises of a faithful God. Without hope, life is reduced to a purposeless
struggle, from precarious birth to certain death, overshadowed always
by meaninglessness and cruel despair. Into that negation and darkness, the Christian hope bursts with the revelation of eternal purpose
and the promise of eternal life. In consequence, all human experience
grows in value and in significance.
      Such are the dimensions of Christian living. By the faith He im-
plants, the love He inspires, the hope He kindles, Christ ushers the
little, individual soul into the wider and fuller life of the Kingdom of
God. Given so great a Christ, the most obscure and handicapped soul
finds enrichment and freedom. At Colossae, self-styled teachers were
claiming to offer more than the apostolic gospel could achieve. You

know better than that, Paul implies, for already life has been immeasurably enlarged for you in Christ. If you want more, you will find it in Him. For the more central the all-sufficient Christ is in your life, the richer and more wonderful will be your Christian experience.

That liberating, enriching experience within the soul may, again, be said to be Christianity, at any rate on its subjective side. Yet here, too, Paul adds something more:

The Miracle of the Church

Out of enriched and emancipated people, the all-sufficient Christ has built His church in distant Colossae. And the church is a third factor in Christianity, something more than the presence in Colossae of a certain number of individual Christians who occasionally meet together. For the church in every place is part of the total body of Christ, a local shrine in the whole temple of the Holy Spirit, a particular group within the complete household of faith. The emergence of that divine society in any new locality has about it always the nature of miracle.

When a Colossian named Epaphras returned from Ephesus to his inland hometown with the Christian faith burning in his heart, others quickly caught his excitement and shared his experience. Those who believed immediately found themselves one: they came together, and they stayed together, because things dearest to their hearts they held in common. Though Christian experience is individual in its impact, it can never remain solitary. *There is only one Christ; we have to share Him or do without Him.* But if we share Him, He will not allow us to stand aloof, independent one of another: He binds us in mutual loyalty, in service, and in memory of His death until He come.

So the saints at Colossae found themselves to be not an assortment of individuals but a faithful brotherhood in Christ, with a common Father. As this letter reveals, they stood in close relationship to their sister churches, while their hospitality toward Christian travelers on the Lycus Valley highroads was becoming known—Paul mentions their love to all the saints.

In every way the little coterie of believers was displaying all the marks of the true church of Christ. The one universal church had emerged in a limited, local situation by its own inherent and infectious power, as part of the continuing miracle of the gospel. Devoutly, with a sense of wonder, and in spite of all its weaknesses and faults, Paul gives thanks for—a Christian church.

This is Christianity in operation. Paul is not concerned to provide definitions, but he has indicated in swift phrases what must be included in any adequate description of the faith we hold. The central focus of all is Christ, in His saving fullness. The immediate fruit of His grace is the Christian, in the fullness of his character and experience. Thus the church emerges, in the purpose of God, in the fellowship of those who are made one by being in Christ and in one place.

So Christ plans to redeem the world.

2

The Word of the Truth of the Gospel
COLOSSIANS 1:5b-6, 23

The two most compelling energies in all human experience are the expulsive power of a new affection and the explosive power of a new idea. "Ideas are . . . forces," said Henry James; "ideas have legs," echoes a familiar slogan, and all history has been described as the adventure of ideas. Great ideas and great personalities are the controlling factors of civilization, and the great personality is often the great idea personified. The story of Christianity is no exception.

Neither Christians nor churches are created by accident. They do not emerge of themselves from the social milieu of any generation, nor fall unheralded from the skies. The creative agency can always be identified: "the word of the truth of the gospel." The power that convicts of truth and kindles life is the power of the Holy Spirit; the means He uses is the good news of Christ, the record of divine redeeming events, interpreted in the light of prophecy and confirmed in the testimony of transformed men.

Such facts-plus-interpretation-plus-testimony comprise the power-packed gospel that exploded in the apostolic world. At once, therefore, after recording his constant thanksgiving for the significant changes wrought in his readers, especially for their triple liberation into larger life through faith, love, and hope, Paul mentions the source of all that they have known—"the word of the truth of the gospel."

Paul seems to mean that faith and love are sustained by the Christian's eternal hope, already laid aside in heaven; and of that hope they first heard in the message of Christ brought to them by their faithful pastor-evangelist, Epaphras.

To expound the content of this life-changing, liberating gospel will take Paul four chapters. Here, as soon as it is mentioned, Paul provides a stimulating description of the Christian message as its effect might be observed by a spectator, watching the gospel at work in the ancient world. He seizes upon three striking facts.

It is a gospel with universal appeal

Powerful ideas are not always popularly received: they may be very limited in appeal, as new medical techniques are limited to specialists, new scientific theories to the few capable of grasping them, philosophic or artistic "schools" may have far-reaching influence although the number who appreciate their real intention may be small. Sometimes, indeed, the main attraction of a new theory or doctrine may lie in its exclusiveness. It will fascinate some just because it is understood only by a distinguished coterie of the well-informed; there is sometimes as much of pride as of persuasion in the vehemence of new converts to some startling fashion of thought.

This was exactly the situation at Colossae. A novel philosophy was sweeping through intelligent circles in Asia Minor. It claimed to be the most advanced, and most intellectual, of all religious doctrines, and offered salvation by knowledge, by divine secrets not to be understood by common people. For them, the elementary ABCs of ordinary Christianity must suffice: but for the truly educated and intellectual was reserved a mystic wisdom known only to the initiated, exclusive to the enlightened "spiritual" few. Those few, inevitably, became intensely proud of their privileges.

With this pretentious nonsense Paul has no sympathy at all. The gospel is for every man. Paul is debtor to the wise and the unwise, to the cultured Greek, the provincial barbarian, and the half-savage Scythian, to the slave and to his master, impartially. He will warn every man, and teach every man, that he may present every man mature in Christ, because his gospel addresses every man in his essential humanity and his individual need.

"The word of the truth of the gospel," Paul says, "has come to you, as indeed in the whole world . . . ." It is no man's private property or exclusive right; it panders to no intellectual snobbery or conceit of knowledge. For all the message is the same, for philosophers at Athens or prostitutes at Corinth, for civil servants at Philippi and Jewish leaders at Thessalonica, for superstitious pagans at Derbe, and a cultured audience in the synagogue at Antioch. A highly cultivated doctor such as Luke, a runaway slave such as Onesimus, a wealthy Jewish landowner such as Barnabas, and Erastus the city treasurer of Corinth all share the same gospel: ". . . I determined not to know any thing among you," writes the apostle, "save Jesus Christ, and him crucified" (1 Corinthians 2:2).

The gospel's universal appeal is one of its surest claims to be of God. The marvel is—if it were not too familiar to be noticed—that men and women of all races and ages, of all types and backgrounds, of all levels of education and of none, find in the story of Jesus, in His parables and miracles, His teaching and promises, His invitations and warnings, His life, death, and resurrection, something that tugs at their heartstrings and rings true within their souls.

The procession of the saints through the ages is a motley cavalcade: soldiers, mystics, poets, scholars, monks, philosophers, statesmen, artists, cobblers, builders, explorers, nurses, teachers, gentle ladies and women of the city streets, of every people and tongue and nation. For the language of the gospel, of love, suffering, forgiveness, hope, is universal language; the spectacle of the gospel, of innocence and love cruelly rejected but winning through to victory, has universal power; while the person of the Saviour, filled with gentleness and strength, with truth and grace, with holiness and compassion and never-failing understanding, is a universal magnet. It is a message for the world, as He is Saviour of the world: it is my faith, as He is my Saviour— but never mine alone.

It is a gospel with fruitful effect

". . . By their fruits," says Jesus, about true or false teachers and doctrines, "by their fruits ye shall know them" (Matthew 7:20). Whether any man or church or sect has the truth of the gospel or only thinks it has, is soon settled: What kind of people are being produced? Those who abide in Christ bear fruit, while the fruitless professors of religion are pruned away. The fruitless tree, needing to be dug about and fed for one last chance; the fruitless fig tree by the wayside, symbol of the disappointment Israel had been to God; the fruitless seed, choked or shriveled in early growth or stolen by passing birds—all figure in Christ's teaching. For fruitfulness reveals life, and the quality of fruit shows the quality of the tree that bore it.

At Colossae the gospel had produced people of faith and love and hope, showing hospitality and consecration. They had once been estranged, hostile in mind, doing evil deeds, but now they are reconciled, to be presented to God as holy, unblameable, irreproachable. They have been made alive in Christ and raised from the level of their former life; they have put off the old nature with its ways, and have been renewed. For them, now, Christ is all in all, their hope of glory. All this Paul firmly asserts. He challenges—what *fruit* has this new, deceitful philosophy that so fascinates your minds?

He brooks no merely intellectual argument; he will not parry words with phrases, making debating points with glib tongue on themes that remain, when all argument is over, mere notions in the mind. He challenges with the test of Christ for false teaching or true: what quality of living does it produce? What fruit does it bear in character and conduct? Concerning the new ideas gaining ground at Colossae, his own reply is brusque and scathing—It is "empty!"

Of the gospel he claims that it is bearing fruit and *growing*. Colossae was a young church: how long would the gospel's effectiveness last? Are they so soon to leave the truth as it had been taught by Epaphras for some specious novelty of doctrine? The picture of soon-grown, soon-withered seed on shallow ground haunts the mind: quick effects may quickly disappoint. It is fruit that increases which demonstrates enduring truth.

This is always the final test of the value of the teacher's message and of the hearer's faith, that it goes on bearing fruit in character, experience, and positive good, increasingly through the years. The gospel of Christ never grows stale.

Says Alexander Maclaren:

> There is no need to leave the Word long since heard in order to get novelty. It will open out into all new depths, and blaze in new radiance as men grow. It will give new answers as the years ask new questions. Each epoch of individual experience, and each phase of society, and all changing forms of opinion will find what meets them in the gospel as it is in Jesus . . . . Beautiful is it when the little children and the young men and the fathers possess the one faith, and when he who began as a child "knowing the Father" ends as an old man with the same knowledge of the same God, only

apprehended now in a form which has gained majesty from the
fleeting years as "Him that was from the beginning."

By that inherent power of increasing fruitfulness, no less than by
its universal appeal, the Christian gospel proves its claim to be divine.

It is a gospel which imparts grace

Closer still to experience, of the Colossians and of ourselves, is the
glorious fact that the gospel of Christ is the medium, or means, or vehicle, of grace. It is not only about the grace of God in Christ: it im-
parts grace to all who believe. That is its final proof that it is divine.

The Graeco-Roman world was a difficult environment in which to
preserve innocence of mind, purity of life, sweetness of temper. It was
a hard world, indeed, in which to survive, and hardest of all, perhaps,
in which to rise again when once one had fallen. How should one find
forgiveness and renewal, be rescued, reformed, remade, when once
the licentiousness and corruption, the cruelty, pride, and selfishness
of paganism had darkened conscience and undermined character?

It was as a hope of moral redemption that the gospel broke into
that heathen world, as the power of God unto salvation. Even in corrupt, ill-famed, permissive Corinth, men were "washed . . . sanctified . . . justified in the name of the Lord Jesus and in the Spirit of
our God" (1 Corinthians 6:11 RSV). By the grace of God in Christ,
any man might start life afresh, renewed in his very soul.

So the Colossians had known the grace of God—the grace that redeems; the grace that keeps, amid all the pressures and temptations
of the world; the grace that proves sufficient in face of suffering and
disappointed prayer; the grace that makes men gracious when all else
in life might make them bitter, envious, and resentful.

So runs Paul's stimulating description of the gospel that makes men
Christian: universal in appeal, fruitful in effect, grace-imparting in its
transforming operation. These qualities demonstrate its truth. No new
teaching could carry higher credentials, convey greater blessing, than
the Word the readers had heard from the beginning. It is not a new
gospel we need, but a new understanding of the gospel we first received—for that is, and ever remains, the word of truth.

"This is for real, man!" Paul declares in effect. "You know the
grace of God *in reality.*" This is no cobweb of ideas cleverly spun in
novel—or even in orthodox—patterns: this is everlasting truth shap-

ing experience, redeeming character, fashioning society, determining history. The events we tell really happened, in Bethlehem, Galilee, Judea, the Easter garden. The meaning of what happened has been tested and confirmed a million times by all sorts of people in count- less different situations, and always they testify to love and pardon, grace and redemption, God's presence and promise and hope, renew- ing their lives. "This is for real . . . ."

But no man need take another's word for it. Test it for yourself. Discover the truth in your own experience. Commit your life, now, just as it is, to the saving grace of Christ, and find for yourself "the word of the truth of the gospel." You will soon join the excited crowd streaming from Samaria, in the wondering confession, "Now it is no longer because of your words that we believe, for we have heard for ourselves and we know that this is indeed the Saviour of the world."

3

A Faithful Minister of Christ
COLOSSIANS 1:7, 8, 4:12, 13

Whether business, pleasure, or some purely domestic occasion first brought Epaphras from his home at Colossae on a visit to Ephesus, about a hundred miles away, we do not know. But while there, he was drawn to the stimulating lecture sessions conducted by a magnetic little man in the Lecture Rooms of Tyrannus. An eloquent Jew, with a wealth of knowledge and afire with conviction, daily drew crowds to public exposition and argument, setting forth the story of Jesus of Nazareth in the context of Jewish prophecies, and as a means of forgiveness, peace with God, enlightenment, assurance, moral renewal, and everlasting life.

Epaphras was attracted, persuaded, convinced, converted. Back home at Colossae, he immediately set about sharing the news, and the joy, that had come to him at Ephesus. From his preaching arose the Colossian church; from his part in its founding followed his pastoral leadership of the little group. They had first learned the gospel from Epaphras, and now looked to him for further teaching, counsel, and encouragement.

With the growth of the work, the emergence of new problems, and the spread of novel, challenging ideas contrary to the first Christian teaching, the new pastor evidently became aware of his own limitations. He returned to the apostle, with a report on progress and with a request for advice. While he stayed with Paul, this letter of counsel was carried to Colossae by Tychicus. In it Paul three times commends Epaphras, in warm, affectionate, wholehearted terms well calculated to ensure a welcome and full authority for the pastor on his return.

Had there been serious opposition to Epaphras, or a rival for his pastoral office, Paul must have said more, and spoken more sharply. More probably, the specious speculations gaining some acceptance in the church, claiming to offer a more enlightened, more advanced version of Christianity, had called in question Epaphras' competence and authority. Paul therefore throws around him the mantle of his own complete approval, as a man, a teacher, and as a representative of apostolic authority—"on our behalf."

In so doing, he reveals the kind of Christian minister whom an apostle can approve.

He will be an affectionate colleague: in Paul's language, a "beloved fellow servant." There are many signs that Paul was a lonely man, and affectionate by nature. His conversion to Christianity probably involved a breach with his family, and the new circle of brethren and sisters conferred upon him in Christ was correspondingly dear. Someone has counted over sixty colleagues and comrades mentioned in Paul's letters, and he often coins words to express a shared Christian experience and loyalty, as "fellow-servant, fellow-soldier, fellow-worker, bound-together, buried-together, made-alive-together, raised-together, knit-together" from this short epistle alone plainly show. Whenever Paul opens his heart, or pleads that others will uphold him in their prayers, we feel his dependence upon the goodwill and encouragement of his friends in Christ. His eager appreciation of the congenial companionship of Epaphras is typical of the apostle.

But more is here than the individual's need of fellowship. The Christian worker, and especially perhaps the Christian pastor as leader and "first among equals," must ever be in some sense set apart from the work which occupies other people, and insulated from some of their temptations. The very qualities that make him leader make him different. Any sincere sense of vocation, confirmed by discovery of talent, spiritual gift, divine blessing, must constitute a peculiar temptation to him, to think of himself more highly than he ought to think. And that very weakness, if indulged, incapacitates him for ministry to other Christians.

In the same way, such a leader must have his own clear convictions about how he should work, what he should preach, by what methods the work of Christ may best be done. But those very convictions seem to imply that those who work, or preach, or organize, in other ways must be wrong. Yet it is quite certain that no man can be a true servant of Christ if he is unable to get on with other Christians.

For Christ was unwilling to work alone. Deliberately He chose twelve that they might be with Him: amid their variety, their slowness, their obtuseness of mind and dullness of spiritual understanding, He moved with infinite patience. He would take them with Him, all the way—even into the Garden of His agony, and feel sorely let down when all they could do there was to fall asleep. Moreover, they were chosen not as a dozen individuals to work alone, but as a company, a new twelve of Israel. He sent them out at first in pairs, not singly; and at the end, warned them that only in their mutual loyalty and love would men recognize that they were His disciples.

If Jesus could cooperate with the twelve, waiting for their comprehension with such forbearance and welding them into one, so must we with our colleagues. No group in which our Christian service is set could ever be more difficult to get on with. To be an affectionate colleague, a man must have small conceit of himself, a high valuation of other Christians, a constant sense of the privilege of being in Christ's service at all, a realization of his own debt to those who served Christ in his life, and a deep reverence for the cause above all considerations of his own performance in it, or his personal importance, or any reward.

The minister who would win apostolic approval must show this Epaphras quality of being good, and easy, to work alongside.

He will be, also, and at the same time, a faithful servant of Christ. It is not always easy to be a warmhearted colleague *and* a faithful servant of Christ. Some ministers find it easier to be friendly than to be faithful and might argue that it is more important; others feel it more important to be faithful, even at the cost of friendship, and perhaps find it easier, too. Epaphras earned Paul's approval on both points.

To be faithful, a man must have convictions and principles to which, when need requires, he will be humbly steadfast even at the cost of disagreement with those he admires and values. To be faithful to Christ means that in any crisis of choice, a man has settled already that his prior loyalty is to Jesus. To be faithful to Christ may mean continuing to preach (as Epaphras had done) the original, authoritative truth of God even when current fashions of thought run counter to evangelical teaching and pretentious substitutes are offered in terms that appeal to intellectual pride and moral laxity.

To be faithful to Christ may mean (as again it did for Epaphras) being constant in loyalty and friendship toward some whom others despise as foolish, weak, unspiritual. It may mean, as for Epaphras, standing to the task and the responsibility even though one's ability is questioned, one's competence criticized, one's authority opposed. Being an affectionate and friendly colleague does not mean submerging one's conscience to the average, common level of insight, or refusing to go forward unless the crowd goes with you.

Such faithfulness calls for clear perception of the real issues in ministry to others; it demands courage and the ability to detach one's judgment from the natural bias of friendship and see truth and right impartially; it calls for readiness to speak forthrightly and act with integrity but always in humble appeal to what is right, not to one's own authority or opinion.

If a man has no such strength, or the will to use it, he will never achieve leadership, and any group of people committed to his charge will fall apart in dissension. If he asserts his convictions and principles in any overbearing or intolerant way, then he will destroy fellowship altogether. The middle course may not be easy, but in practice it proves easier than it sounds. For earnest Christian hearts, truly concerned for the work of God, always appreciate the humbly faithful leader and minister of God who speaks and acts with integrity and love. They will often thank God for his fidelity.

The minister who would win apostolic approval must certainly manifest the Epaphras quality of *loyalty to his people*. One cannot imagine the loyal Paul having any patience with pastoral disloyalty.

A minister must be sufficiently identified with his people, and with all of his people, to know their spiritual needs and understand their problems. Epaphras had come to Paul to seek counsel, and that meant reporting on the state of the church, revealing specific areas of concern, isolating trends and causes and dangers. The report was suffi- ciently clear and serious to evoke a letter of detailed teaching and strong counsel. Epaphras knew his church and his people; he has his ear to the ground, is aware of what is going on, what people are saying and thinking, and why. He is a poor pastor who stands so far from his flock that he is constantly taken by surprise at what they do.

Yet it is evident, beyond all doubt, that Epaphras spoke well of his people. Paul is moved to thanksgiving by what he hears, of their faith, and love, and hope, and hospitable friendliness, and "love in the Spirit." Plainly the pastor has not denigrated his friends or spoken ill of his people in any way—an acute temptation, when the soundness of your own teaching has been challenged and the adequacy of your own leadership has to be defended! But away from home, the loyal pastor has only good to speak—as a man will speak only well of his family circle and their ways when he is over his own doorstep, what- ever discipline he must exercise indoors.

Perhaps the secret of such loyalty is the ability to see people's faults and dangers without losing sight of the fact that they are won- derful folk. Whatever Epaphras needed advice about, whatever warn- ing or rebuke Paul must write—these Colossian Christians *were* Christians, and that was miracle. The loyal pastor never lets his de- tailed disappointments or fears obscure the major truth about his fellow members, that they are the salt of the earth, brethren and sis- ters in Christ, people for whom Christ died.

The minister who gives such loyalty, knowing his people intimately, ever speaking well of them, thinking highly of them whatever the problems, will surely receive like loyalty in return. He who with- holds it will surely want it.

Finally, the minister who would win apostolic approval must be *a pastor in prayer.* The deepest expression of Epaphras's loyalty to his people is emphasized in the last chapter of Paul's letter: away from his church, the pastor is constantly in prayer for his flock, iden- tified with them in the presence of God.

The prayer he offers, that the Colossians may stand "mature and fully assured in all the will of God," arises directly from his insight into the real dangers and uncertainties that trouble his people. To pray properly for others, one must take the trouble to understand their need. The hard work to which Paul testifies may look back to Epaphras's pastoral duties when at Colossae, but it seems to emphasize

the deep concern, even distress, which moved his prayers. His intercession was no mere pastoral duty or function: he prayed not only
about them, certainly not against them, not only with them, but as
one of them.

This is the inevitable *priestly* aspect of ministry. Too often attention is concentrated upon the priest's "right" to speak to men on
God's behalf, and his consequent authority: in New Testament
thought, emphasis falls instead upon his privilege of speaking to God
on behalf of men—with their names and needs heavy upon his heart
as a pastoral breastplate. Whatever we think about the right terms
and titles for this experience, it is an inescapable element in Christian
service in other lives.

One remembers Paul's moving cry, "Who is weak, and I am not
weak? Who is made to stumble, and I do not burn with shame?" (*see*
2 Corinthians 11:29). And his anguish for the Galatians—"My little
children, with whom I am again in travail until Christ be formed in
you!" (Galatians 4:19 RSV). Such glimpses of his emotional identification with his converts lend depth to those recorded prayers, and
the many references to prayer, that occur in his correspondence. Of
church after church he can record, as he does of the church at Rome,
"without ceasing I mention you always in my prayers": only the
letter to Galatia fails to mention such pastoral and priestly intercession for the readers.

Can we doubt that our words of counsel and warning to our people
take on an altogether new note when we have prepared ourselves by
praying for them? A firmer authority, a keener perceptiveness, a
deeper sympathy, a more watchful concern, and far fewer blundering
interventions where we can do no good, are the pastoral rewards of
faithfully "remembering earnestly in our prayers" the people God has
given us for our care.

These are not perhaps the first qualities we would have listed in
seeking a minister of apostolic stature. Is nothing to be said of his
competence in Christian work, of his knowledge of the gospel, of his
gifts and spiritual power and personal dedication? Much might be said.
But Epaphras had already shown the truth of his message, as Paul
testifies; fruitful signs of spiritual power had been evident, too, at
Colossae; while his toil, his intercession, and his presence now with
the apostle for their sake, express his dedication to his work. Of all
this the Colossians should be well aware.

It is of the added excellences that Paul speaks with such warmth of praise—perhaps because they are comparatively rare. Given a true message, competence, and zeal, the special qualities of grace that enable a man to be among his fellow Christians an affectionate colleague, a faithful servant of Christ, a loyal pastor, and an interceding priest, are of immeasurable value to any group eager to stand together and work together for Christ.

There are not many modern churches that would not gladly and gratefully invite Epaphras to become their minister!

4

A Pertinent Prayer
Colossians 1:9-12

One might even call it "an impertinent prayer." It is surely disconcerting to have an apostle pray publicly that you might be wiser, and to have the prayer recorded for all time. That Paul should intercede for Christians everywhere is not surprising; nor that he should turn the polite blessing to the gods and good wishes to the readers, conventional in all ancient correspondence, into a truly Christian thanksgiving and prayer. But that he should ask, and repeatedly, that the readers might be wiser, more knowledgeable, more understanding, seems—to say the least—unflattering.

Yet some among the Colossian Christians would say a fervent *amen*. Paul's prayer strikes exactly the note that would appeal to them. For to that inland township, standing where several highways met to pierce the Cadmus range and thread eastward to Palestine and Persia, westward to Ephesus, Greece and Rome, many passing travelers brought news and ideas from many places to stimulate an already mixed population of natives, Greek colonists, and Jewish forced immigrants. Among the new fashions of thought spreading across Asia hard on the heels of the gospel was a strange combination of philosophy, superstition, and ritual magic. In its Christianized form, it offered an "advanced" spiritual wisdom and experience to

those "initiated" into divine secrets, and many found the bait ir-
resistible.

Paul will presently warn of the dangers of this intellectual self-
deceit and snobbery, and will insist that in Christ the Colossians have
all the treasures of wisdom and knowledge and a full assurance of
understanding. Here, his prayer is that they will realize that—realize
to the full the wisdom they already possess, and go on to be filled
with knowledge, wisdom, and understanding. His request could
scarcely be more pertinent.

Paul's prayer is qualified, however, in ways less likely to appeal
to any intellectual conceit among the Colossian members. The knowledge Paul has in mind is not philosophy, or information about
mystic visions and occult secrets: it is the knowledge of God's
will—less pretentious, but infinitely more practical and important.
The wisdom he has in mind is not the fleshly wisdom of this world,
which he will describe as an empty falsehood based on human traditions, but spiritual wisdom that enables a man to find his way
among spiritual realities and receive the fullness of spiritual life.

Least welcome of all to the intellectuals is Paul's insistence that
the purpose of mental endowments is not personal satisfaction, nor
superior statue within the Christian fellowship, but "that you may
lead a life worthy of the Lord" (RSV). Knowledge or wisdom for
their own sake do not interest the apostle; he suspects that they
tend to puff up Christians with false pride. But for the Christian
understanding which nourishes worthy Christian behavior, Paul has
high regard. This is what he asks for the Christians at Colossae.

And first, for moral understanding:

It takes far more than wisdom to produce great character. But
in an age of confusion, contention, denial, when customary rules
of behavior are despised, traditional codes challenged, and all kinds
of moral experiment advocated as evidence of adulthood and pro-
gressiveness, moral understanding cannot be despised. The new
fashion of thought infecting the church at Colossae bred just such
confusion about right and wrong as confronts our own age, and
Paul is concerned that they shall be given sound Christian instruction, clear Christian insight, and intelligent Christian common sense.

(1) Paul himself would once have turned, for the knowledge of
God's will, to the Mosaic Law and the Jewish Torah. But he had

learned the insufficiency of external codes, the uncertainty and confusion that arise from the endless adjustments and reinterpretations
required to keep any written code up-to-date. He had come to know
that the letter killeth.

In place of the directives of the Law had come the revelation of
God's will in Christ, in word, and deed, and above all in the inspiration of His indwelling Spirit. On all moral questions, Paul
would appeal wherever possible to the words and example of Jesus,
and where that was not possible, to the leading of the Spirit. We
may watch him following this pattern of counsel as he answers questions put to him by the church at Corinth. Such knowledge of the
Lord's life and teaching, together with the inner guidance of the
Spirit, made up for Paul "the mind of Christ" by which he directed
all his life. For us, both this knowledge about Christ and the inspired direction of the Spirit are enshrined in the New Testament
Scriptures: and Scripture and the Spirit remain the source of all
sound, and safe, instruction in Christian living.

(2) But instruction in Christian tradition and ideas is not of itself enough to illumine the Christian's way. The inherited truths
must become light within the mind: instruction must awaken insight and another's teaching pass into personal perception of the
truth. A man must see for himself the rightness of the behavior
advised; must perceive for himself the true scale of priorities when
duties conflict; must catch for himself the vision of the end toward
which God leads him.

Such light, insight, perception, vision, cannot be imparted. They
arise in the mind which is not only soundly instructed but willing to
respond in faith and obedience to what it learns. This is spiritual
wisdom, a maturity of understanding which makes the Christian
aware of the Lord's will, sometimes without being able to cite texts
or to provide arguments for what he sees so clearly. Anyone privileged to number among his friends an old saint wise in years and
"intimate" with God, will know exactly what Paul covets for the
Colossians.

(3) Yet even sound instruction and matured wisdom are not sufficient to direct behavior without careful and detailed application to
the real situations confronting the Christian. Each life knows its
own circumstances, problems, temptations, its own frustrations, want
of talent or resources or friends; the extra difficulties caused by the

wrongdoing of others, or by the sin within one's own heart. Christian character emerges only when the ideal presented in Jesus, and the moral wisdom garnered through the years, issue in a *yes* or *no,* an *I will* or *I must not,* in specific situations.

This calls for the third capacity for which Paul prays, Christian common sense, or judgment. Paul's own word for *understanding* implies this ability to bring theoretic principles to bear upon concrete problems. Not all who discourse eloquently on Christian ideals are good at finding their way through the problems presented to Christian conscience by a secular and permissive society. Some seem, indeed, to be incapacitated for firm and clear decision by their familiarity with large, wide-ranging theories and principles. Christian wit and sincerity can sometimes find their road, relying on the Lord, where much learning goes astray.

But knowledge, wisdom, and common sense together make for moral understanding and fine living: though all three, of course, are not enough without the grace of Christ and the power of the Spirit. So Paul prays, secondly, for:

The moral maturity which such moral understanding may confer.

The fine living which Paul has in mind is a life "worthy of the Lord, fully pleasing to him" (RSV). To be worthy of the Lord, of God, of the gospel, of our calling—all Pauline expressions—sounds an impossible ideal. Paul plainly means that while we can never be worthy, in the sense of *deserving* Christ, or the gospel, we can and should strive to be worthier of Him who saved us in our worthlessness. To be *fully pleasing* to God seems equally beyond our hope. Yet who, loving Christ, would ever be content not to be worthy, not to be fully pleasing, to Him who is above all praise?

As if that description of Christian ideals were not enough, Paul spells it out in four tremendous phrases. To be worthy and pleasing to the Lord means:

(1) *Bearing fruit in every good work*—not in certain particular and isolated forms of virtue which come easily to us, or which we happen to admire, but in the whole circle of Christian goodness, in deed, and attitude, and word. This often requires paying attention especially to duties and qualities of character which do not come readily

to us. It certainly means we must not be content with limited, and easily satisfied, or conventional, ideals but must be ever striving forward to completeness, to the fullness of the stature of Christ.

Yet the echo here of Paul's great word about the fruit of the Spirit suggests not so much the goodness produced by some effort of attention, but the goodness that flows, as Christ's did, from the quality of life within. It is the full and spontaneous outflow of life made good at its source. In the end, moral understanding and a worthy life must show their value in sheer goodness—in deeds and days that are good for someone, good for something, and in every sort of way.

(2) To continue to be worthy and pleasing will mean *increasing in the knowledge of God.* No character remains sound or fruitful without unceasing progress. Some timid souls fear that progress in faith and experience must imply leaving behind one's earlier precious lessons of faith, one's simpler and more childlike thoughts of God. Dreading apostasy, they refuse to leave behind the elementary principles of the doctrine of Christ and press on to maturity.

Yet in spiritual as in natural things, childhood's ideas can be true and valid for childhood without remaining true and valid for middle life and old age. The man must put away childish things if he is not to remain childish. First steps in Christian life proceed on the assumption that every true prayer is granted, every sincere soul is shielded from want, from care, from suffering; that full divine blessing is granted at once if we have faith enough, and every faithful gospel sermon will draw and convert crowds—and so on.

Experience teaches deeper things. Unanswered prayers sift our praying. The adversity and hardship of true children of God, the suffering of the innocent, the high cost of discipleship, the inexorable conditions of blessing and of spiritual power—all have to be reckoned with. The soul must grow up, must increase in its understanding of God's character and ways, learning His faithfulness and love in dark days as well as in light, if faith is to be matched to the realities of life. Only then will character remain steadfast when hopes and dreams crash round the breaking heart; only then will the house of life stand firm and unshaken when wind and flood have passed. There is no need for fear. God's grace and faithfulness grow only more wonderful as experience explores His greatness and finds that of His mercy there is no end.

(3) In such a world as this, a life worthy of the Lord and fully pleasing to God needs to be *strengthened with all power according to His glorious might*. Much moral idealism fails through its inability to kindle the strength of mind and will necessary to moral achievement. Aspiration is not enough; perspiration is rarely successful—earnest determination may impose discipline but it cannot produce the beautiful soul; only inspiration, the inbreathing of power, is adequate to achieve moral victory and joy.

That victory, Paul adds, must include—besides attainment—fortitude and patience for the hard way and the exhausting test. Life is not often a simple matter of knowing the right and deciding to do it. The pressures of the world, the sin within the self, and the inescapable cross have to be faced with courage and conquered with power.

But the strength is not only demanded—it is offered; we are not required to be strong, but to be strengthened. And that, not according to our capacity for resolution, our little resistance to evil, or even our despair: the only limit is "according to his glorious might" (RSV). Given a humble and receptive faith, there is no end to the strength infused into those who strive toward life worthy of the Lord. Paul prays that the Colossians may discover the unsuspected might which fills, encompasses, and sustains those whose lives flow with the current of God's high purposes, and tend toward the goal that Christ has set before them.

(4) The prevailing emotional tone of such a life will be one of *giving thanks to the Father*. At least five times, and possibly seven, in this short exhortation, Paul returns to the thought of gratitude, in varied connections: here, he urges thankfulness that God has given to sinners the qualifications necessary to share the inheritance of the saints in light.

Basically, Christian thankfulness is the constraining motive, the undergirding sense of immense and undeservable privilege, which replaces all other motives for religious life. It replaces fear as the reason for obedience; it is the substitute for self-righteous pride, for the selfish pursuit of reward, for the accumulation of merit, or the calculating repayment for wrongs done that sometimes makes the guilty turn religious. When the divine gift and invitation rest entirely upon God's grace, the only appropriate and sufficient response open to man is unabating gratitude.

In that unfading awareness of being unpayably indebted to God's grace, of having been privileged beyond all possibility of deserving, lies the emotional tenor of the mature Christian character. All is done, obeyed, aspired after, freely dedicated, or gladly renounced, in deep thankfulness for so great salvation already enjoyed. If the Colossians —and many modern Christians—really possessed such a sense of the mercy that has made their lives so different from other men's, the temptation to seek substitutes for the gospel and some fancied new spiritual excitements in other religious camps would never arise.

However high they soar, Paul's prayers always keep their feet firmly on the ground. A deep and ever-increasing comprehension of the will of God, issuing in a life on all sides worthy and well-pleasing, fruitful, enduring, mature, and grateful, is as much as any man can ask, or hope for, for himself or for others. Yet it rests at last on things as obviously needful as Christian instruction, Christian insight, and Christian common sense. And such, after all, is the least that any Christian would ask for his friends, or for himself.

The Fullness of Christ

5

Preeminent With God
COLOSSIANS 1:13-15

Christ is at once the glory and the scandal of Christianity. Only the most violently anti-Christian seriously challenges the lofty idealism of His teaching, the beauty and strength of His character, the moving drama and historic significance of His life. For believers, half-believers, and wistful would-be believers alike, Christ is the Rose of Sharon, the Lily of the valley, the fairest of ten thousand, the Man above all others.

But Christ is not content with compliments, nor is Christianity content with heartfelt memorial tributes to a great life. The Christian claim is that Christ is entirely unique. Peter speaks for the whole Christian church: "There is salvation in no one else, for there is no other name under heaven given among men by which we must be saved" (*see* Acts 4:12). So does Christina Rosetti:

> None other Lamb, none other Name,
> > None other Hope in heaven or earth or sea,
> None other Hiding-place from guilt and shame,
> > None beside Thee.

> Lord, Thou art Life tho' I be dead,
> > Love's Fire Thou art, however cold I be:
> Nor heaven have I, nor place to lay my head,
> > Nor home, but Thee.

"None beside Thee"—that is the scandal of Christ's claim.

For the world has many teachers, leaders, saints, and not a few self-styled redeemers. What is so special about Jesus? Of course, every faith thinks its founder unrivaled, but that is simply loyalty tinged with fanaticism. There are many ways to heaven, we are told, many sides to truth, many great pioneers, even in religion. Why cannot Jesus take His place in the gnostic's endless chain of spiritual beings, in the Roman and the Hindu pantheon along with others? Why this dogmatic, exclusive, even arrogant claim that Jesus is unique?

For Paul, that question was settled, as for Paul all theoretic questions were settled, by practical Christian experience. He had first confronted Jesus at Damascus Gate as the risen Christ, to whom at once he made complete and never-to-be-qualified surrender, crying "Lord, what wilt thou have me to do?" (Acts 9:6). From that insight, his thought moved backwards to the preexistent Christ in the form of God, who thought it not a thing to be grasped to be equal with God; and forward to the Christ who must reign until He has put all enemies under His feet. Paul will say much in this short letter concerning Christ, some of it breathtaking in its range of thought, depth of faith, vigor of expression, and far-reaching implications. But all springs from his experience of Jesus as first and foremost Lord of life and Bringer of salvation.

Paul has been giving thanks for the Colossians' Christian experience, praying for their growth in understanding, recalling especially the need to be constantly grateful for all that Christ has done—and there his mind takes fire. In a rush of kindling thought, at least fifteen tremendous statements about Jesus tumble one over the other, winding splendidly to the fine expression, "that in all things he might have the preeminence." That thought, the utter, absolute, unquestioned supremacy of Christ over all imagined rivals, fills Paul's mind. Christ is unique, alone, incomparable, preeminent. Our whole experience of salvation through Him demonstrates there is "none beside Thee."

The crucial issue, of course, is whether Christ stands nearer to God than all others. All truly religious experience is experience of God, and it is here Paul's great assertions begin: Christ is without peer, or rival, or comparison, in all that relates to God. Paul piles claim upon claim to buttress his affirmation, that in all that concerns man's experience of God, Christ stands in lonely, unshared preeminence.

(1) *Christ is God's Son, preeminent in rank.* He was declared to be the Son of God by the resurrection from the dead, Paul maintains. ". . . I live by the faith of the Son of God" (Galatians 2:20), he confesses. "God sent forth His Son" is the heart of Paul's gospel— "He spared not his own Son, but freely gave him up for us all." Luke suggests that this was the first note Paul struck in his preaching in the synagogues at Damascus, "Jesus is the Son of God" (*see* Acts 9:20). So here it is the first emphasis he makes: Jesus is the Son of God's love.

In all such phrases, the unequalled dignity of Christ is being declared. He is the One in whom, according to all Hebrew ideas of sonship, God's own character is reproduced, and God's own life finds full expression. In Him, God Himself has entered human history. Originally in the form of God, Christ emptied Himself, and was made Man —such is the grace of the eternal Son. Of no other in all creation could that be said. Christ stands unrivaled in rank, as the only begotten Son of the everlasting God.

(2) *Christ is God's beloved, preeminent in relationship,* the one upon whom, in a unique way, God's love is set. "His own Son" as Paul expresses it, or "Son of his love," or quite simply "the beloved." The gospels suggest part of the meaning in the words, "Thou art my Chosen, in whom I am well pleased"; John gives us, for the deeper part of the meaning, the vivid metaphor ". . . the only begotten Son, . . . in the bosom of the Father . . ." (John 1:18).

No one is nearer to God than is Christ. John's phrase really means that as a disciple leaned on the breast of Christ, so Jesus leaned on the breast of God. The whole story of Christ's prayer life, His inexpressible intimacy with the Father, allows us a glimpse of that unfathomable unity of the Son with the Father out of which Christ speaks to us. ". . . no man knoweth the Son, but the Father; neither knoweth any man the Father, save the Son, and he to whomsoever the Son will reveal him" (Matthew 11:27). Such is the preeminence of Christ as Bearer of God's word and power: He comes among us out of a uniquely intimate and personal relation to God, His Father —and ours.

(3) *Christ is God's king, preeminent in rule,* exercising divine authority. Behind the brief reference to the "kingdom" of the Son lies a wide field of Paul's thought. To Christ God has given the Name that is above every name, that at the Name every knee shall bow. So to confess with thy mouth Jesus as Lord and believe in thine heart that God has raised Him from the dead, is to be saved. Christ is God's vice-regent. The Kingdom of God so familiar in the gospels is brought nearer to most of us in the epistles as "the Lordship of Christ." Jesus is not only Messiah to Israel, but King of men, Prince of life, and Lord of all who believe.

Once we dwelt in the land of darkness and the shadow of death, ruled by the prince of darkness. But God has delivered us, Paul says, from the kingdom of darkness and translated us into the kingdom of

His beloved Son. As, long ago, Israel had been translated from the kingdom of Pharaoh into the land where God alone was King; as more recently, many Colossian Jews had been translated from other settlements into their present home by Antiochus; so the Colossian Christians have experienced their exodus from the kingdom of sin and their translation under the rule of Christ.

So in authority over Christian minds and hearts Jesus is preeminent: beside Him there can be no other. He alone wears the laurel, bears the crown, wields the scepter—Jesus King most wonderful and Conqueror renowned. He rules in the kingdom of love.

(4) *Christ is our divine Redeemer, preeminent in responsibility.* He it is who is charged with all God's saving purposes for mankind, and who remains sole bearer of their tremendous cost. He only could unlock the gate of heaven and let us in. Others have taught the world wise and wonderful truth; others have labored, explored, struggled, sacrificed, for mankind. But none other could redeem. Here, beyond all question, Christ stands without peer. To deny this is not merely to deny Christ's uniqueness, but to deny redemption itself: to affirm redemption is to know that in all history only one life, one love, one sacrifice ever has achieved, or ever can achieve, that supreme miracle.

Paul, as he writes, still has uppermost in mind the practical needs of his Colossian readers. For among them the uniqueness of Christ was being challenged by novel ideas about many intermediary beings who "filled the fullness"—bridged the gap—between God and men. Allied with this was the notion that salvation was essentially a matter of knowledge, of being initiated into divine secrets. Redemption, these teachers said, was for those intellectually capable of receiving it: the only redemption that mattered was enlightenment of mind. Paul replies bluntly, flatly, that *redemption is the forgiveness of sins.*

That is the need, the desperate situation, from which man needs deliverance—his sin and its consequences in himself, in society, and in human destiny. From that predicament, only Christ incarnate, crucified and risen, can possibly save. He bears the sin, the responsibility of redemption, the cross that redeems—and He bears it alone.

(5) *Finally, Christ is the image of God: preeminent in revelation.* No man has seen God at any time, as John makes clear: the only begotten Son has declared, has "expounded" God to men, has made God understood. In Christ the invisible God is made visible, the incomprehensible is expressed in human terms. So the message concern-

ing this unveiling of the unknown God is called "the gospel of Christ, who is the image of God."

The graven image of Caesar on a Roman coin, the carved image of the beast described by the seer of Patmos, and even the mental image conveyed by a word portrait, are all part of the meaning of Paul's significant word. Christ is the living representation of God; in Him God opens His heart to us; in Him the mind of God becomes a spoken word; in Him the will of God is unresistingly personified.

Prophets and psalmists, poets and philosophers and saints, have in their turn and in their degree helped men to think about God. But who, that has fully appreciated the broken half words and quarter words (as Martin Luther called them) in which others have tried to express God, will doubt that in Christ we have the Word made flesh, spelled out, made crystal clear, compelling, memorable? He is not yet another pious seeker after God, reporting hesitantly to others what he thinks he has found: He comes forth from God seeking men, and declaring the mind and will, the character and purpose of God as one who is Himself divine. His perfect revelation of God cannot be proved: it can only be perceived by believing, grateful hearts. But those who so receive it thereafter cry with Peter "Lord, to whom else shall we go? For Thou hast the words of eternal life" (*see* John 6:68).

Such is the glory of Christ as Christian experience bears witness. In rank, relationship, rule, redemptive responsibility, and revelation, Christ is in a class by Himself. In everything that relates to God, He is alone, unique, preeminent. In Him we know God, see God, and God touches us. As Harry Emerson Fosdick said years ago, Christ is the near end of God; the point at which the measureless ocean of the Godhead washes our shores.

Before his letter is finished, Paul will insist that an adequate view of Christ's fullness is the answer to the poverty of soul within us. But it is also the answer to much of the confusion around us. In an age of dissolving standards and fading traditions, when cleverly posed questions are taken for answers, and the challenge to ancient insights is itself mistaken for wisdom, to be confused becomes the badge of modernity, and agnosticism becomes a convenient evasion. Yet if Christ be indeed the self-disclosure of God in human experience, there is no room left for agnosticism. Philip's plea, ". . . Lord, show us the Father" (John 14:8 RSV), has been decisively and authoritatively answered: ". . . he that hath seen me hath seen the

Father . . ." (John 14:9 RSV). On that all practical and worthy
assurance may safely be built. Light has come: men may continue
to love darkness and ignorance if they will, but now it is self-chosen.
In the face of all that Christ has done to bring God to men and men
to God, agnosticism is no longer untaught ignorance, but simply unbelief.

As our one world draws closer together in its planetary home
against the vast background of outer space, what notions of God can
possibly satisfy all races and types of mankind? As human knowledge
expands to the boundaries of the explorable universe, and an un-
imaginable future beckons, what conceptions of God could ever
prove adequate, stimulating enough or reassuring enough, as tomor-
row unfolds? Only Christ's vision of God is sufficient; only His revelation of the Father can possibly be reconciled with our understanding
of the universe. A humanist Christ, however sympathetically por-
trayed, will not serve us here, can bring no unique revelation, no
authoritative divine disclosure. Only He who stands over against us
on God's side of the great divide and steps toward us, the unique
revealer and redeemer, unrivaled in all that relates to God, can meet
our need. And such He is:

> True Image of the infinite,
> And God's beloved Son.

6

Preeminent in the Universe
COLOSSIANS 1:16, 17

By a curious, even ridiculous, paradox religion is persistently associated with narrowness—of mind, of interests, of horizons. That is not
only slanderous, it is silly. Only the irreligious, and perhaps the half-
religious, suppose that religion can be kept strictly in its place. The
truly religious man is never satisfied until the whole circle of human
existence, of duty and relationship and vocation, the whole of experience past, present, and future, the whole of earth and heaven, is all

impressed into the service of his faith. He acknowledges no special place for religion—it encompasses everything.

So the Bible begins with the whole earth, the sun and moon, the heavens and the stars, teaming nature and the whole of humankind, all the handiwork and the instrument of God. Nothing is excluded from His power, His purpose, and His glory. So the psalmists declare a hundred times that heaven and earth, the sea and the hills and the valleys, the rocks, the rivers, the pastures, the wilderness, the sunlight and the storm, and all the varied life of shepherds, soldiers, scholars, guides, husbandmen, sailors, kings, and common folk—all tell the tale of divine compassion and care: all contribute to the glory of God.

John's gospel begins with the same unlimited range of faith. "In the beginning was the Word . . . . All things were made by him, and without him was not anything made . . . . In him was life; and the life was the light of men . . . . the true light, which lighteth every man that cometh into the world . . . ." The letter to the Hebrews says the same: "God . . . hath . . . spoken unto us by his Son, whom he hath appointed heir of all things, by whom also he made the worlds" (Hebrews 1:1, 2). And Paul likewise, whether preaching at Athens or writing to the Romans, finds God's handiwork in everything that is.

But it is in the first chapter of the letter to the Colossians that this expansive world-affirming faith of the Bible rises to a towering pinnacle of vision. In a great hymn to the cosmic Christ, Paul stretches our faith to the utmost with breathtaking affirmations about our Saviour in relation to the universe about us. He makes the most astonishing claims, and though his language is that of the first century, the implications of what he says are so entirely contemporary that he might have been writing for our space-conscious generation.

Paul's theme is the preeminence of Christ. As in the experience of Christian men in all that relates to God, so in the universe about us in all that relates to creation, its past and its future, Christ is without rival or parallel or peer. He stands in the universe alone, the unique, supreme, preeminent, cosmic Christ.

(1) In the whole universe, Paul claims, *Christ is first in cosmic time:* "the firstborn of all creation." It is possible that "firstborn" carries double meaning, *prior in time* and also *prior in claim* as the firstborn who inherits. Certainly God has appointed the Son "heir of all things." John's way of asserting the eternal preexistence of Christ—"In the

beginning was the Word, and the Word was with God" does not really go beyond the Master's own prayer ". . . Father, glorify thou me with . . . the glory which I had with thee before the world was" (John 17:5).

That the Saviour appeared in time and history is the central wonder of the gospel; but that He "came," "was sent," "took upon him the form of a servant . . . being found in human form" is the glorious presupposition of His being here. Language fails to express, as imagination fails to picture, what this really means: we only know that Christ belongs to eternity, He *chose* to be in time. He is the eternal, the timeless, Lord.

(2) Of the whole universe, *Christ is the ultimate, cosmic origin:* "for in him all things were created, in heaven and on earth, whether thrones or dominions or principalities or authorities—all things were created through him . . ." (RSV). Again, "the world was made through him" is John's echo of Paul's thought. All things owe their existence to His creative agency; all things bear His hallmark and His signature. As the Christian, and the church, have their existence only "in Christ," so, in a wider sense, only "in Him" does creation itself come to be and remain in being. Christ is Mediator of the first creation, as of the new creation.

It is an astounding claim. Jewish minds were familiar with the thought that Wisdom stood at God's elbow as God fashioned the heavens and the earth. John says that Wisdom was the eternal Word, later made flesh; Paul says that Wisdom was Christ, the Son of God. Some of the Colossians were toying with ideas about an endless chain of spiritual intelligences filling the void between God and the world: Paul lists the supposed names of these lords of the spiritual world, without comment—and almost contemptuously—and then roundly declares that Christ is prior to them all, and above them all. If there are such, He made them! "You name it, He is above it!"

> At His voice creation
>   Sprang at once to sight,
> All the angel faces,
>   All the hosts of light;
> Thrones and dominations,
>   Stars upon their way,
> All the heavenly orders
>   In their great array.

sings Caroline Noel, doubtless with Paul in mind, and John too: "Whatever was made, had life in him." These early Christians showed neither narrowness nor modesty, in their claims for Christ!

(3) Still further: of the whole universe, Paul continues, *Christ is the final, cosmic purpose:* "all things were made . . . for him." In the last assessment, the ultimate goal of all things must be the glory of God: but in that glory Christ shares; while in preparation for that great end, all things fulfill His aims, serve His purpose, and promote His glory. The universe knows no higher end than Christ.

Without Christ in it, all history would be pointless; without Christ, all creation would be without hope, or goal, or destiny. Apart from Him, we can discern within the universal process no purpose, direction, progress or culmination: all seems to go out at last in darkness, cold and nothingness. Christ is Omega as He was Alpha, the end as He was the beginning, the destination of all things, as He was their origin and source. He is the clue to the meaning within the seeming muddle—all things tend to Christ, being made "for Him."

(4) Pursuing his tremendous theme yet more deeply, Paul adds boldly that in all the universe *Christ is the very center of cosmic existence:* "He is before all things, and in him all things hold together." Paul is not now thinking of which came first, Christ or creation, but of which —so to speak—depends on which. And he is asserting that just as all things came to be through Christ and for Christ, so they are held in being by His divine hand: "in him all things cohere, consist, hang together." Could any claim be more daring? The argument at Colossae about where to place Christ in the scheme of things is not so much answered, as silenced!

We can glimpse Paul's meaning if we remember that every single thing that we have ever seen, touched, handled, depended for its existence on something else, that was there before it, that caused it to be. All created things are derived from previous things; they are dependent, upheld by something not themselves. And this includes ourselves: we are not self-dependent, did not give ourselves life, and cannot continue to live except in utter dependence upon others, upon the world, and upon God. Not so Christ, says Paul. He *is,* before all else. Christ depends upon nothing and upon no one, except the Father, the Source of all being. Rather do all things depend upon Christ. In Him they hold together; by Him all things consist, find their inner coherence, and their final meaning. Without Christ the universe is no longer meaningful, or viable: He is its meaning, its coherence, and its life.

Firmly, uncompromisingly, Paul is placing Christ where He belongs. He is not the last and lowest link in some descending chain of spirit beings linking God and men; and not some remarkable but pathetic humanist born before His time, well-meaning but impracticable, and so sacrificing Himself in vain. Christ, to Christian hearts, is the center and source of all existing things, their spring, their meaning, and their end.

(5) Even yet Paul has not quite done: in all the universe, he concludes, *Christ shall yet be the center of cosmic unity.* For through Him all things shall be reconciled to God—"all things, whether on earth or in heaven, making peace by the blood of his cross" (RSV). At the last, Christ will bring this shattered, fragmented, alienated chaos of things to order, to beauty, back to its divine design.

Paul saw the world divided, embittered, at enmity with itself and with God, alienated from the Source of its true welfare, and split into warring races, nations, religions, with each man similarly divided within himself. Everywhere is conflict: the one desperate need is reconciliation. And this is Paul's gospel: God has reconciled us to Himself by Jesus Christ, and beseeches men, through the apostles, ". . . be ye reconciled to God" (2 Corinthians 5:20).

So Paul sees Christ at the center of the universe as the Head and Focus of its unity, bringing all things again under divine control, making peace, reconciling all in its original, primeval harmony. For that day, the whole creation groans in travail until now.

Such is Paul's vision of the cosmic Christ. For a generation probing deeply into space and standing amazed at the immensity of things, such a faith has immeasurable meaning. Over sixty years ago, Alice Meynell rehearsed in beautiful phrases how God has dealt with this "our wayside planet" in the birth, the cross, the resurrection. No other planet knows the story that we know, but neither may we guess in what forms our neighboring planets may have learned to think of God. They may have other messages—a million alien gospels—but earth's testimony to the universe concerning Godhead must always be—a Man!

Poets, like apostles, strain imagination in trying to express the ultimate things of faith. But the sober meaning of their vision, of the Christ who fills the universe, may be expressed in very plain terms. By the *cosmic fullness* of Christ we mean that wherever man goes, on earth or in space, he will still be confronted by Christ's challenge and ideal; we mean that whatever man discovers, on earth or through space, will bear the marks of creative Mind, as Christ has taught us to discern them; we mean that however brilliantly clever man becomes, he will still need the grace of Christ to make him good; we mean that however far man shall penetrate to the horizons of the expanding universe, no immensity of distance, neither height nor depth, shall be able to separate him from the love of God in Christ Jesus our Lord.

For this we firmly believe: wherever in multitudinous worlds still undiscovered God is ever known, it will be through Christ that He reveals Himself. But this too we know: that because He is the universal Christ, making, upholding, guiding, reconciling all things, He embraces all life and all creation. *Because He is behind all things, we can keep Him out of nothing.* All life is His, all truth, all beauty, all goodness; and all that concerns us must be brought into relation with Him. Nothing then is inherently evil—since all was created by and for Christ, and has its being and its goal in Him.

Thus all life is involved in Christian faith and obedience. Religion can be kept to no special corner of a man's life. All things are yours, all things work together for good, all things are of God, and whatsoever things are true and good, pure and lovely, virtuous, honorable and of good report, take their place in healthy Christian dedication. The sphere of creation and the sphere of redemption unite in Christ; for secular as well as for spiritual problems, Christ is the answer.

For the cosmic Christ is Lord of all life, King of the world, preeminent in the universe, and the only Saviour of all.

7

Preeminent in the Church
COLOSSIANS 1:18-20

Strange as it may seem, the preeminence of Christ within His church has not always been very obvious. Christian thought has sometimes been influenced as much by Greek philosophy, Eastern asceticism, and political expediency, as by the insights and imperatives of Jesus. Church government has sometimes resembled the bitter wrangling of ambitious men for place and power more than the rule of Christ. The church's true mission of salvation has occasionally been obscured by her greater concern for her own privileges, discipline, and prosperity. Not once nor twice in Christian history, the world has pleaded with the church, "Sirs, we would see Jesus!"

Sometimes, as in the teaching gaining ground at Colossae, and later in the extremer forms of Mariolatry, the preeminence of Christ is questioned even in the church's doctrine. More often, it is the selfishness, the worldliness, the ambition or cowardice of men that dethrones Christ from His rightful place. Whatever the cause, for the church's own sake as much as for the world's, Christ's preeminence within His church must be reasserted vigorously and repeatedly, as Paul does here.

(1) *Christ is preeminent within the church in His unique authority as its Head.* Christ, Paul said, is the Head of the body; the church's true place is as the body of Christ. Probably our notion of the head as the seat of intellectual direction and control is too dependent upon modern knowledge of the brain and nervous system to represent Paul's thought. The Hebrews spoke, instead, of the thoughts of the *heart*. It may well be that Paul meant simply that Christ is *chief* within the church, an idea expressed later in the phrase, "Head of all rule and authority." Paul undoubtedly means at least this, that the church is subject to Christ as her Head and Lord.

But in ancient physiology the head was already known to be vital to the living body. Wounds to the head were usually fatal; through the head all light and sound entered consciousness, keeping man in touch with life around him; injury to the head often brought darkness, unconsciousness; through the head the whole body was nourished, and by means of it the inner self found expression in speech, laughter, tears, and that character in a face of which the Jews were so aware.

What the head was to the body, Christ is to His church, the vital center, the one essential "organ." The whole Christian society was dependent upon Him, subject to Him, centered in Him. He was indispensable to its organic life, and to its several parts. As the temple without the indwelling deity is a house left desolate; as the branch

separated from the vine is mere tinder for burning; as the body
without the head is a lifeless carcass; so the church that has lost touch
with its head, the living Christ, is a husk, a pretense, a dead tradition
fossilized in an institution, a plaster facade without function, strength,
or beauty.

(2) *Christ is preeminent within the church in His unshared honor
as its Source.* To us that seems obvious: to Paul and his Jewish
contemporaries, it was revolutionary. To say "He is the beginning"
is to transfer to Jesus the glory that for many generations had been
given to Abraham, scarcely shared by Moses. If Christ is the Beginning, then all that preceded Him was preparatory, provisional, and
imperfect; and all that followed Him derives significance from its
relation to Him. To affirm this demanded courage and provoked
hatred.

It implies that the whole movement of God in history led up to
Christ, and the whole purpose of God in history really began at His
appearing. Apostolic Christians were sure that this was so, and they
delighted to declare it. He is the Alpha, they said, the bright morning
star, the dayspring from on high, the author of our faith. He makes
all things new. If any man be in Christ, there is for him a new
creation. Christ is the second Adam, the new Man from heaven, Head
of a new race, who ushers into newness of life.

In slightly different terms but expressing the same essential truth,
these early Christians declared Jesus to be the Prince of life, the
file-leader, the Pioneer. An endearing trait in the matchless portrait,
treasured among the gospel memories, shows Jesus always going just
ahead of the rest, leading the way, breaking new ground, into the
storm, up to Jerusalem, back to Galilee, into the future. The whole
of Christianity may in consequence be condensed into the simple
phrase, "Follow me!"

For indeed Christ was and is the Originator of the church. She
derives her claim to Christian allegiance, and her certainty of endless
endurance, from that one fact: "I will build my church," Jesus said,
and so He did; because of that, ". . . the gates of hell shall not
prevail against it" (Matthew 16:18). From Him directly sprang her
whole life and fellowship, her message and experience, her task and
hope. He *was* her beginning, source of all her memories, fount of
her inspiration, wellspring of her buoyant strength, lodestar of her
conscience, light of her mind, joy of her heart.

And He *is* ever her beginning: from Him her whole life, fellowship, message, experience, task, and hope still spring. Christ is her every new beginning. Only from Him, and in Him, does the historic church find constant renewal, reform, and rebirth. When she loses her first Love, her light goes out, forever.

(3) *Christ is preeminent within the church in His sole glory as risen and ascended Lord.* "He is the firstborn from the dead." Paul appears to mean that that is the ground of Christ's position in the church. It is not alone as incarnate and crucified Christ that Jesus stands at the beginning of all things Christian, and sits as Head within His church, but as the risen and glorified Lord, in whom all Christians live. The church is no merely commemorative fellowship perpetuating a past age and recalling a departed hero: she knows that He to whom all power was given in heaven and on earth is with her always, according to His word.

But the title "firstborn" seems to imply more than the *fact* of Christ's own Resurrection, as first conqueror of death; it conveys also the *promise* that the "firstborn" will bring many sons to glory. He is the firstfruits of all that sleep in Him. So the risen Christ within the church becomes the ground and focus of all Christian hope: through Him the church tastes already a future life, and belongs already to another world. Set within the present world to live, to minister, to evangelize, perhaps to suffer, she yet holds her citizenship in another country, and enjoys a timeless communion.

Paul is always aware of this eternal dimension of the historic church of Christ: but it remains true only so long as she remains the shrine, the body, of her ascended Lord. It is Christ who confers upon the little Christian assemblies scattered through the world this eternal quality; only as He is given His due preeminence in all her life and thought does the church remain the divine society, her standards, her aims, and her reward not of this world but of that which is to come.

(4) *Christ is preeminent within the church in His supreme purpose, to use the church to reconcile all to God.* Paul's sentence breaks under the weight of meaning he strives to express, but the essential point is clear: God was pleased that all the divine fullness should dwell in Christ, in order that all the divine purpose might focus upon Him—namely "to reconcile to himself all things, whether on earth or in heaven, making peace by the blood of his cross" (RSV).

The intention to reconcile, the qualifications of the Reconciler, the means of reconciliation—the cross—and the range of reconciliation—all things—are brought together in that great sentence. The only adequate comment would be the Epistle to the Ephesians, for that letter is, in fact if not in origin, a meditation upon this verse. Paul saw the universe as fragmented, at odds with itself, divided and disintegrating; torn by self-destructive forces of selfishness, rebellion, and sin. The world was falling apart; an inner force of evil was destroying the unity God intended.

But God's plan—says Paul—for the fullness of time is to "unite all things in him." God will sum up all the conflicting elements of the world under one Head, even Christ. The first step in that plan was to create out of many races and types of people one church; the church then became both example and partaker of God's reconciling purpose. Some would be won to the divine unity by the death of Christ; others, possibly, would be subjected to the divine unity by the power of Christ, in the day when He shall put down all rule and authority and might, and God shall be all in all.

One way or the other, the cosmic Christ will unite the warring worlds under divine rule. In that universal task Christ has no rival, no peer, none to share the glory—or the pain. But He deigns to use the church, the reconciled and reconciling fellowship, to be the agent of His cosmic work, provided always that His supremacy and His purpose remain preeminent among His people. Without Christ, the church has no task to do, no power to do it, no hope of seeing it done. He is the Reconciler: He has committed unto us the word of reconciliation, God beseeching men by us, "Be reconciled." But no one else can break the stubborn will, woo the estranged heart, unify the alienated soul—none save Christ. For that reason too, He must remain in unrivaled control of all the church's life.

In all these ways Christ stands preeminent within His church, as He does in the universe and as He does in all that relates to God. But what if those who bear His name fail to accord Him rightful place in their loyalty and love? What are all the claims and theological affirmations about the peerless, paramount Christ of God, if He is not first in adoring hearts? Paul leaves no doubt that such is his real purpose—that in every Christian mind and soul Christ might have the preeminence.

Two moments in his own life illustrate what Paul meant by that evocative, but sometimes sentimental, phrase. Returning from Miletus to Judea, aged and weary but still intrepid, Paul found at Tyre

Christians who told him "through the Spirit" that he should not proceed to Jerusalem. Yet on the appointed day, they go forward. At Caesarea, the warning is repeated by Agabus, who mimes the binding of hands and feet that the apostle will undergo at Jerusalem, and again in the name of the Spirit warns against proceeding. The Christians at Caesarea join in pleading with Paul, only to meet his demand, "What are you doing, weeping and breaking my heart? For I am ready not only to be imprisoned but even to die at Jerusalem for the name of the Lord Jesus" (Acts 21:13 RSV). And when he would not be persuaded, they ceased, saying, "The will of the Lord be done." To a man for whom Christ was "in all things preeminent," to die for His name was far more an incentive than a threat!

Later, in prison and daily awaiting the verdict which meant life or death, Paul confesses that he cannot say which he would choose. To live would mean fellowship with Christian friends, and further fruitful service for Christ; to die meant to be with Christ, which was far better. So, he says, "Which I shall choose, I cannot tell . . . . For to me to live is Christ, and to die is gain" (Philippians 1:21 RSV). Beside the claim of the preeminent Christ, all else is devalued— all personal ambition, desire, self-seeking, are dwarfed before the supreme loyalty to the unrivaled Lord.

In the end, the high doctrine must nourish high devotion. Only when we think adequately about who Jesus is do we give Him the rightful place within our lives. On the other hand, only when we give Him rightful place in all things is what we profess to believe about Him seen to be true. Jesus Himself asks, ". . . why call ye me, Lord, Lord, and do not the things which I say?" (Luke 6:46).

8

Preeminent in Christian Experience
COLOSSIANS 1:21-23

"And you!" How abruptly Paul returns from wide-ranging specula- tion on the cosmic significance of Christ to confront squarely the little group of Christian believers in the valley town of Colossae!

"And you!"—of what value are high-flown, exuberant affirmations of faith concerning Christ and God, Christ and creation, Christ and the future, if in our own individual lives Christ has done nothing very much?

"And you!" Paul has been thinking of God's ultimate purpose, to reconcile all things through Christ, to reduce to order and unity a world, a whole universe, divided against itself and fast falling into warring elements. Suddenly he recalls the argument, the illustration, the living instance of his meaning that lies close at hand. The supreme experience which Christ had brought to the believers at Colossae had been to find themselves at one with God, at peace within themselves, at home in God's world. That is Christian reconciliation. The universal purpose, ranging far beyond time and human imagination, had already transformed *them:* "And you . . . hath he reconciled."

Paul often returns to this great theme of reconciliation through Christ. But there is probably no passage in his writings where it is more succinctly, more completely, summarized.

Here, first, is *the threefold alienation which makes Christ's reconciliation necessary.* Before Epaphras, their founder-pastor, had brought them the Christian message, the Colossians had been "estranged, hostile in mind, doing evil deeds." Each word has weight.

(1) Some among Paul's readers would understand only too well what Paul meant by "estranged, alienated," for they remembered coming as unwelcome immigrants into an alien community when Antiochus transplanted their homes and families into a foreign town. Stephen uses the same word of Abraham's children, *aliens,* in a land belonging to others, deprived of rights and of freedom, banished from where they belonged. "Paul does not say 'aliens' as though it were an original condition, but 'alienated' as having become so," says Alexander Maclaren, summarizing in a sentence man's lost, estranged condition.

Inevitably, the language recalls the shutting of the gates of paradise on the primeval pair, banished for disobedience; the loneliness of the prodigal Jacob, ill-used in a strange land in consequence of his own wrongdoing; that other prodigal son, unsheltered, rejected and lone, far from his father's home through his own folly and sin. ". . . your iniquities have separated between you and your God" (Isaiah 59:2), declares an Old Testament prophet; "Remember," echoes the apostle, ". . . you were . . . separated from Christ, alienated from the commonwealth of Israel, and strangers to the covenants of promise, having no hope and without God . . . far off . . ." (Ephesians 2:12 RSV).

(2) It is part of the irony, and the desolation, of that estrangement from God that man always blames God for it. He will not believe that he deserves banishment: the fault lies with God's "wrath," the harshness of divine law, the injustice of life, the hopelessness of the human predicament. Man turns against the God whose love he has outraged; the alien becomes an enemy alien, bitter at heart, "hostile in mind." The gulf of estrangement widens as man refuses every overture of love, every invitation to return; he disbelieves every promise of mercy and erects barricades against every approach of God—then blames God for his self-isolation and despair.

(3) Paul completes the appalling analysis: man's enmity toward God finds expression in deliberately evil deeds, so hardening the hostility, confirming the estrangement, poisoning all thoughts of God with feelings and fears of personal guilt. The sense of distance, the attitude of enmity, and the memory of transgression constitute a religious, psychological, and moral alienation from all that would ensure man's highest welfare and his eternal destiny. In three directions at once his need is desperate.

Here, secondly, is *the threefold divine reaction which makes Christ's reconciliation possible:* "You he has now reconciled." Here is all the gospel—the divine initiative, as the basis of faith's grateful response; the finished work, to which man can add nothing by his own labor or merit; the present enjoyment, for the Colossians knew that this reconciliation through Christ was already the center of their lives.

(1) Reconciliation was not a process to be painfully pursued through darkness and the long night of a soul seeking its way back to an elusive God. It is no reward offered for merit sedulously accumulated by discipline and good deeds. No need here to measure one's length on the ground in some humiliating pilgrimage to Rome or Mecca or the Ganges, desperately striving to win or buy or deserve divine favor. *The work is done:* the gulf is bridged, the barriers are down, and God invites us home.

(2) Lest any at Colossae should begin to think of many spiritual mediators between God and man, or of salvation through fancy

intellectual theorizings and divine secrets, Paul at once anchors this divine act of reconciliation firmly to Christ's incarnation and His life among men, to His "body of flesh." We, too, in careless moments, think of our relation to God as wholly subjective, a private concern of the inward motions and moods of the soul. In truth, all our knowledge of God, approach to God, and joy in God, are now conditioned by Christ's revelation of His character and purpose. Only as the estranged, defiant, embittered soul turns to God in Christ, won over from resentful hostility by the quality of Christ's life and the immeasurable patience of His love, can any reconciliation take place. Alienated men do not rethink God for themselves: they discover God in Christ, the Christ of Galilee, and are drawn home to the Father whom He perfectly reveals in word and deed.

(3) Yet not in word and deed alone, but "by death." All things are reconciled as Christ "makes peace by the blood of His cross." It is not man's misunderstanding, merely, that needs to be dealt with, but his sin and guilt. The life and ministry of Jesus reveal the true character of God, whom man's hostility persistently misrepresents; but it is the death of Jesus which makes possible reconciliation between God and sinners. The separating sin is borne away in the sacrifice of Christ; a new covenant between God and men is established in His blood, shed for many for the remission of sins. As the arms of the cross spread wide to embrace all men, so they reach up and down to draw heaven and earth together. Unerringly Charles Wesley perceived the double reconciliation at the cross:

> Vouchsafe the eye of faith to see
> The Man transfixed on Calvary,
>   To know Thee, Who Thou art—
> The one eternal God and true!
> And let the sight affect, subdue,
>   And break my stubborn heart.
>
> The veil of unbelief remove;
> And by Thy manifested love,
>   And by Thy sprinkled blood,
> Destroy the love of sin in me,
> And get Thyself the victory,
>   And bring me back to God.

So is man's desperate threefold need met by God's threefold initiative in Christ—to reconcile, to reveal, and to redeem.

But here again is *the threefold consequence that makes Christ's reconciliation effective:* He presents us holy, blameless, and irreproachable, before God.

(1) The opposite of being separated, at a distance from God, is to be brought near, to be introduced again to the presence of the Most High. It is to step again within the lost garden; to return from the far country to the Father's home; as Peter says, "Christ died to bring us to God" (*see* 1 Peter 3:18). To Paul this was the almost incredible consequence of salvation. Again and again he wonderingly records that being justified by faith we have access—through Him we have access by one Spirit unto the Father—we have boldness and confidence of access through our faith in Him.

The torn veil of the Temple, at the moment when Christ died, symbolized for all time that the way into the holiest was at last made free and man could stand again unafraid in the presence of his God. For Paul, this is the experienced meaning of reconciliation, to be accepted in the Beloved, to be granted access to the standing ground of grace, to be received into fellowship, no longer at enmity but welcomed by the Most High.

(2) In all probability, the qualifying words elaborate this welcome. Christ reconciles us through His death in order to present us to God *holy,* acceptable to His pure majesty, not to be banished again—for if God be for us, who can be against us? And to present us *blameless,* unimpeached before the court of heaven—for who shall condemn us, when it is Christ that died, and rose again, and intercedes for us? And again, to present us *irreproachable,* with no charge sustained against us—for who shall lay anything to the charge of God's elect, when it is God that justifieth? Doubtless Paul means also that we shall be so presented at the end of time in the eternal courts, made fit for the inheritance of the saints in light. But we do not wait for reconciliation—we have it now: its daily, continuous reality lies in being at all times accepted in the Beloved.

(3) The former "enemy alien" is *presented* at court. Paul was so *presented* to the governor Felix; the bride is so *presented* to her husband; the infant Jesus was so *presented* before God within the Temple. All these suggestions are in the word. But the last, with overtones of acceptance at a monarch's court, with the ruler's face turned "to shine upon you," is probably nearest to Paul's meaning. Paul's plea is not that the Colossians shall prepare for judgment day, but

that they shall enjoy now the daily fellowship of their reconciled God, and not let false speculations about some vast impassible gulf rob them of that joy. The plea is still needed, though for many of us it is not false teaching which robs us of close intercourse with God, but neglect of the opportunity which Christ's reconciling work has placed within our reach.

So Paul adds *the threefold condition upon which the continuing enjoyment of Christ's reconciliation depends:* ". . . provided that you continue in the faith, stable and steadfast, not shifting from the hope of the gospel. . . ."

Stable, steadfast, be not moved—these are building metaphors that recall words of Jesus about houses built on rock or sand. But the Colossian district was volcanic, subject to strong and frequent earth tremors, and the figures would have dramatic appeal: stand firm in the faith when all around you is shaken; hold fast to Christ when all else is carried away. At the heart of a well-founded, soundly constructed Christian character will be the constant renewal of reconciliation, as Christ presents them ever and again to God His Father.

To continue in the faith means more than to continue to be orthodox. Paul is certainly concerned about the deceitful philosophy being dabbled with at Colossae; he knows it will mislead into spurious "experiences" and weak character. But it is for the quality of their lives that he is primarily anxious, and he would have them steadfast, stable, unmoving in their daily adherence *to Christ* who first, and continually, reconciles them to God.

That is the force of "And you . . . hath he reconciled. . . ." When all else is said about the cosmic glory of the eternal Christ, which has been filling Paul's thought, still the most wonderful thing of all is—that He has brought us back to God. He Himself, our Lord and Friend and Saviour, is the center and spring and vehicle of all that is deepest and most divine in our own experience. My spiritual life endures at all only because He is its foundation, its resource, and its reward. Ever and again, in every hour of penitence, of need, of shaken faith and wavering loyalty, of loneliness or sorrow, *He presents me again to God,* unafraid, accepted, welcomed into favor because He lived and died for me.

That is why He is and must remain preeminent in Christian experience. None can share His place within the hearts that know His reconciling work.

"And *you,* too, hath he reconciled . . . ."

9

A Christ-Centered Ministry
COLOSSIANS 1:23c-29

Paul was the least egotistical of men. Some men find it easy and congenial to talk about themselves; some introduce themselves into conversation on every possible occasion. Others do it only when some serious purpose demands it, and then with self-conscious apology. Paul needed occasionally to assert his authority, even to defend his apostleship, and once or twice to bear a personal testimony. But he is never quite at ease in referring to himself.

Yet it was well that he should explain his concern for the church at Colossae. He had neither founded the church nor visited it—yet he sends counsel and warning. He will point out that he was called to be minister especially to the Gentiles—and that includes Colossians; and he will urge that his pastoral concern is all the greater, and not less, for those whom he does not know *in person*. But there was a third reason for his personal concern.

Paul says he was especially charged with making the word of God fully known, and that word centered in the person of Christ. When the Colossian pastor, Epaphras, reported that some strange ideas current at Colossae tended to question, or to obscure, the unique greatness and sufficiency of Christ to save, then Paul, the apostle of Christ and the lover of Christ, could not help but be stirred. In addition, scholar and Jew though he was, Paul had long felt himself to be debtor to every man, Jew and Gentile, wise and unwise, slave and free man. The distortion of the gospel, by some at Colossae, into a philosophy for some spiritual or intellectual elite of "advanced" Christians, simply made him angry.

Thus Paul would be false to his commission and to himself if he ignored what was happening at Colossae; he is not interfering, but he is concerned. And though he speaks so personally, he in fact says little about his experience, his achievements, or himself, but much about the meaning of the Christian ministry, and about the hallmark of the Christian ministry, which is Christ.

The meaning of a Christ-centered ministry—servitude. "Of which I became a minister," Paul says twice. The first time, he means "I became a minister of the gospel"; the second time, "I became a minister of Christ's body—the church." A few lines earlier he describes Epaphras as a minister of Christ.

(1) In this three-dimensional calling of the Christian minister lies a three-point loyalty. He must be true to the gospel, in his thinking, preaching, teaching, counseling. He must be true to the church, in all his activity, his intercession, his use of his time and gifts. He must be true to Christ, in his inmost spirit and dedication, his holiness of life, his integrity of method, and his purity of aim. To be fruitful in the gospel, profitable to the church, and faithful to Christ his Lord, is a commission challenging enough to draw the best out of any man.

For the ministry of the gospel involves skill and study and patience; the willingness to go on exploring truth in a teachable spirit of inquiry; the wisdom to apply the general truth to specific cases and problems with all the care, insight, and compassion needed for the cure of souls. The ministry of the church will demand energetic striving—Paul's word is borrowed from the athletic Games of Greece; it will require some administrative skill and forward leadership that still remembers to keep the followers in hail. The ministry of Christ will demand above all that a man's work be Christ-centered and filled "with all the energy which Christ mightily inspires."

(2) Yet even more searching than this triple obligation is the precise meaning of the title itself. Through the centuries, the word *minister* has gathered to itself considerable reputation, reverence, authority, even affection. It is attended with processes of appointment, insignia of office, distinctions of dress and of status that together confer on the title an aura of great dignity, approaching sometimes to majesty. But *minister* in the New Testament is a word of menial origin: it denotes the house servant who waits at table. It is used of all who serve their fellows—as Paul immediately adds, it is "for you." The title implies not dignity but lowliness of status; it connotes not authority but subjection.

The insignia of the Christian ministry in the New Testament are the towel and the basin; its example is in Him who came, not to be ministered unto but to minister, and to give His life a ransom for many. Its spirit is that of the Servant of the Lord, who must work the works of Him who sent Him, and finish His work. Its confession is, "I am among you as one who serves" (Luke 22:27 RSV). The sense of great privilege remains: Paul speaks of having a "stewardship" committed to him, as to the bailiff or manager in the parable, entrusted with the distribution of the Lord's "riches" in His name. Nevertheless, the essential and determinative conception of Christian ministry is plain: it is the service of the Servant of the Lord.

(3) Behind that phrase lies all that is deepest and most penetrating in our thought of Christ and of Christian work. Centuries before Paul, Israel's profoundest thinkers realized that divine election of a "chosen" people was for *service* among the nations, not for superiority. Israel as a whole failed to rise to that inverted glory; only a remnant would be the Servant People, to bring the whole nation to God. Later even that expectation failed, and One was seen to stand alone—the Servant of the Lord.

The Servant would not strive or cry or raise tumult in the streets. He would be marred beyond recognition; He would have no beauty that men should desire Him, but would be despised and rejected of men, a man of sorrows, who would make many righteous by bearing their iniquities. Taking the form of a servant, through three crowded years of exhausting days He lived only to serve the footsteps of His fellows, and fulfill for them the commandment received of the Father.

This divine tradition of servitude determines the attitude, approach, and motivation of a Christ-exampled ministry. The title *minister* means just this—one appointed to serve as Christ, the Servant, has served him. Paul's whole point is that in writing to the Colossians at all he is but fulfilling his servitude. He is obeying the truth he believes, as a servant of the gospel; he is attending to the spiritual need of Christians, as a servant of the church; he is executing the commission laid upon him, as a servant of the Servant-Christ.

The outward pattern of the Christian ministry corresponds to its inward inspiration.

The hallmark of a Christ-centered ministry is—Christ. He reviews in turn the subject, the sphere, the suffering, the secret, and the success of the ministry, and says that each is simply—Christ.

(1) The *subject* of the minister's work, certainly, is Christ: "Him we proclaim, warning . . . teaching . . . every man" (RSV). The

minister has only one theme, Christ in His fullness, and only one aim —to bring the fullness of Christ to bear upon the need of his people. In the last resort, Christ is his solution to all problems, his authority for all pronouncements, his theme for all occasions. Not that uttering the precious Name works as some Christian incantation, making awkward circumstances and complex problems disappear: to proclaim and apply Christ to any soul's need may be a searching, prolonged, and clinical process, sending a man back again and again to ask what Jesus would say to this question, what Jesus would do in this situation, how Jesus would have supported this inadequate soul. The answers may not be obvious, and obedience to them may be costly, in time and in resources. But we have no alternative answers. Where Paul determined not to know anything else, we just do not have anything else commensurate with the modern problem, save Jesus Christ and Him crucified. Him we proclaim.

(2) The *sphere* of the ministry is the body of Christ, by which phrase Paul emphasises the extra dimension which the church possesses beyond all other groups, societies and fraternities. She is more than a circle of friends, a fellowship of kindred minds, a means of mutual support and teamwork: she is the one instrument on earth by which the life of the ascended Lord finds constant expression. As at Damascus Paul discovered that to persecute Christians was to persecute the Christ, so he had learned that he who serves one of the least of these Christian brethren serves Christ also. Whatever their failures, immaturity, divisions, even hostility toward himself, Paul remained "ourself your servant"—because in the last resort he served not men but Christ in men, the Body of Christ. That has sustained many a fine ministry with patience, endurance, and hope, through repeated human disappointments.

(3) The *suffering* involved in Christian ministry, when it is real suffering and not self-pity, when it arises from faithfulness and not from self-righteousness, censoriousness, or hypocrisy, is a sharing of the sufferings of Christ. The words in which Paul says this are among the most obscure in the New Testament, but it is clear that Paul thinks of the toil, affliction, hardship and danger involved in his missionary travel, resistance to opposition, and evangelistic pioneering, as fellowship in Christ's pain. "I bearing about in the body the dying of the Lord Jesus. . . ." Comparatively few in recent decades have been called to such an experience, though those who have suffered

in prison cell, mission outpost, or concentration camp, have borne splendid testimony. Yet the truth stands: a Christ-centered ministry cannot evade the cost of faithfulness. The Christ we serve was no popular demagogue, no idol of the multitude, but a lonely revolutionary on a hideous cross. "The servant is not greater than his Lord" (John 15:20).

(4) The *secret* of the ministry is, *Christ in you.* The pagan religions, the Greek sects, the Dead Sea communities, even Judaism, all claimed their mysteries, their wisdom exclusive to initiates. Christianity, too, has its knowledge hidden from the wise and prudent, but revealed to babes, its understanding of Christ unveiled not by flesh and blood but by the Father. But Paul insists that the mystery is for every man, an open secret, a rich and hopeful secret, promising recovery of the glory which Adam lost. *Christ in you* is the secret of the good life, of spiritual enrichment, of moral transformation, of effective ministry, and of everything else. Richard Crashaw recalls the humble centurion:

> Thy God was making haste into thy roof
> Thy humble faith and fear keeps Him aloof:
> He'll be thy Guest, because He may not be;
> He'll come—into thy house? No, into thee.

Christ in you is the incentive, the strength, the renewing inspiration, the quiet joy, of minister and people alike.

(5) The *success* of the Christian ministry lies in the quality of people it produces: and who is to judge, but Christ Himself? The aim is to present every man, mature in Christ, to Christ for His approval. As Christ reconciles us, presenting us holy, blameless, irreproachable to God His Father, so the task of the minister is to forward that work in every man who assents, till every man is presented mature in Christ. The end in view is no mutual admiration among an advanced and select circle, but acceptance with Christ. So to present Christ to men and men to Christ is the only measure of success in any Christian work; to see it happening, and receive the Lord's approval, is for the minister accolade enough.

Who is sufficient for these things? Amid the pressures and confusions, the ambitions and false assessments of the present age, it is difficult for young men even to want such a career—or, if they want it, to keep their faith in its practicability and power. One sufficient answer is the ordaining word of Christ our Lord: "Ye have not chosen me, but I have chosen you, and ordained you, that you should go and bring forth fruit . . ." (John 15:16). If anything further could be added, it might be the penetrating remark of Luke: ". . . the Lord appointed other seventy also, and sent them . . . before his face into every city and place, whither he himself would come" (Luke 10:1). To be chosen and sent by Him where He Himself would come —that is a full story of every Christ-centered ministry.

10

Completing the Sufferings of Christ?
Colossians 1:24-29

A Bible Study

Some passages of Scripture, clear in their general intention, raise almost unanswerable questions when examined in detail. To be dogmatic, or argumentative, about what they mean is foolish; a reverent, tentative exploration is the only profitable approach. One such passage is Colossians 1:24-29, where Paul explains how he comes to be writing to the Colossian church about their faith and progress, although he had not visited them. He is led to say several things about the Christian ministry and his own place within it, one or two of which sound very odd indeed.

To begin with what is clear:

Paul presents *a wonderfully balanced view* of the Christian ministry, and of Christian service of any kind.

(1) He begins with suffering and ends with toil, yet he emphasizes the immense privileges of Christ's service—how great the riches of the glory of the message; how great the "energy which [Christ] mightily inspires . . ." within those who work for Him; how exalted the stewardship committed to his trust and the divine office given to him. It is easy, amid the frustrations and disappointments of Christian

work, to overlook the compensations, the affection of fine colleagues, the privilege of a pulpit, the opportunity of leadership, the ready-made circle of friends, the opportunity of a task worth putting yourself into, and in some cases the opportunity to earn one's living directly in line with one's highest calling as a Christian. No man could ask for more.

(2) Paul balances the high sense of being set apart as someone called and commissioned, with the sense of being a servant of the church, commissioned *for others,* and sent to "every man." Paul has in mind those at Colossae who claimed to be superior to others: he insists that he is set apart from ordinary work but not from ordinary people. Every Christian worker is sent to "every man"—to those he likes and to those he finds unlikeable; to gifted and enjoyable people and to the obscure and inarticulate; to young and old, to the spiritually mature and to the weak and tempted; to the responsive and the unresponsive, the appreciative and the critical. The Christian leader may enjoy his exalted responsibility and opportunity, but his service is for all sorts and conditions of men.

(3) Paul likewise balances the inward, incommunicable depth of Christian truth, the things that cannot be taught but only discovered for oneself, with the necessity to communicate, to witness, that every man may know the secrets known to faith. Every preacher, pastor, teacher, and friend of youth knows this tension:

> Oh could I tell ye surely would believe it!
> Oh could I only say what I have seen!
> How should I tell or how can ye receive it,
> How, till He bringeth you where I have been?
>   —FREDERICK W. H. MYERS

In the end, a man must make his own discovery of the truth of the gospel. Only the inward light of the Spirit can make the truth shine. We cannot indoctrinate men and call them Christians: we can but lead them to their own discovery of the riches and the glory of the open secret, which is Christ in them, their only hope.

Thus far, Paul's balanced view of Christian service is expressed with great good sense, with candor, and with gratitude.

But Paul has mentioned also *the suffering involved in the service of Christ,* in surprising terms that raise difficult questions. "In my

flesh I complete what is lacking in Christ's afflictions for the sake of
his body, that is, the church . . ." (RSV). What can that mean?

Can Paul mean that the suffering of Jesus for mankind was some-
how insufficient, and is completed by the meritorious sufferings of
apostles, saints, martyrs? Such an idea appears to contradict everything which Paul, and the whole New Testament, affirm about the
finished, sufficient, unrepeatable work of Christ, "once for all," in
atonement for the sin of the world.

It is true that Christ suffers, in sympathy, when His body the
church suffers, as Paul learned at Damascus: but would Paul "rejoice"
in Christ's continued suffering, or regard his own suffering as in this
way adding anything to complete Christ's total of affliction?

It is true also that, in some sense, the contradiction and rejection
which Christ suffered in the days of His flesh are continued in the
experience of the church, as Christians share His mission in an unbelieving world. But is this "filling up that which is lacking in Christ's
afflictions"?

Two far-reaching scriptural insights may afford some light. One is
the conception of a collective Son of Man, as the "one like the Son
of Man" (Daniel 7:13), is Israel as a whole. The Servant of the
Lord, too, is in some passages either the whole people or a remnant
representing the whole people. Is Paul thinking, in some such way,
of a collective or corporate Christ, Head and body together, suffering
together? Does he mean that his sufferings go to complete the afflictions of the "total Christ"?

The other insight concerns an appointed total of birth pangs, or
"woes," which must be endured before the messianic kingdom can
be established. Does Paul mean that his sufferings make their contribution to that sum total of pain still to be undergone before the
day of Christ's kingdom? Both these suggestions read a great deal
into Paul's words; we must examine his exact expression more closely.

(1) It is well to get clear what Paul's words mean before discussing
the whole statement. By "sufferings" Paul means, literally, unpleasant
experiences of all kinds, misfortunes, hardships. The "afflictions of
Christ" mean His tribulation, distress, the result of being under pressure; the word is not used by Paul of Christ's *death*. The "toil" to
which Paul later refers is "labor to the point of weariness." "Striving"
is a word from the Greek Games, meaning "contending for a prize,"
struggling to succeed. Neither word suggests death; the passage recalls
Paul's many references to ill-treatment by mobs or local authorities,

imprisonment, want, hardship, famine, persecution, nakedness, peril, and sword. If here he refers to imprisonment at Ephesus, then Paul as he writes is passing through the most fierce and despairing affliction of his life, as the opening of his second letter to Corinth makes plain.

It seems clear, therefore, that Paul's thought is not of some mystical, or theological, or theoretical, "sharing of Christ's crucifixion" but of actual and literal suffering, which he is undergoing as the price to be paid for faithful service of Christ.

(2) If now we look at Paul's whole sentence, we notice the deliberate balancing of two thoughts: "Now I rejoice in my sufferings for you, and I complete that which is lacking of the afflictions of Christ in my flesh for His body's sake, which is the church." Paul's order of words is somewhat disguised in smooth translations. Paul did not mean, it appears, "the afflictions of Christ for His body's sake"; it is Paul's own sufferings that are "in my body (flesh) for His body's sake." His sufferings are not deserved, or accidental, or criminal, but truly "afflictions of Christ"; and Paul is glad that the pain of his own individual, physical body benefits the whole Body of Christ, of which he is a part.

(3) Whatever is "lacking" is said to be made up by Paul's own personal suffering. Evidently, it is not Christ's own afflictions which are incomplete—or how could Paul's complete them? Nor did Paul complete the church's sufferings: they continue. It is Paul's sufferings, that is, Paul's participation in Christ's sufferings, which are incomplete, and which are brought nearer completion by his present afflictions. When Paul wrote to Philippi, he declared that he was pressing toward such complete fellowship with the suffering Christ as the goal of his spiritual striving. His present afflictions, he now writes, are bringing him nearer to a life completely conformed to die as He died, in the fellowship of His suffering, that he might attain the joy of sharing also in His resurrection.

(4) If this interpretation fails to give the expected weight to the phrase "the afflictions of Christ" it is probably because (a) we think "afflictions" mean death, which Paul never so describes; (b) we wrongly take together phrases which Paul kept separate, and think of "the afflictions of Christ for His body's sake" as Christ's atoning death. Paul means his own afflictions for Christ's sake, borne in his own body on behalf of Christ's body, the church. Paul may well be

using a phrase borrowed from the erring teachers at Colossae, although it does not express perfectly what he means; we might, for example, put the words in single quotes, or translate it as "filling up that which is—as they say—'lacking in the afflictions of Christ.' "

Thus, in describing his ministry Paul mentions his suffering for Christ, but he feels no self-pity, pleads no sympathy; instead, he rejoices in suffering.

(1) Because it is borne for the sake of the church. No value is here set upon affliction for its own sake, ascetically, or morbidly. As when he wrote to Philippi, Paul is glad when what happens to him serves to advance the gospel. All persecution undeservedly suffered is to this degree vicarious: "the blood of the martyrs is the seed of the church."

(2) Paul rejoices in his suffering because it is a participation in the sufferings of Christ, a contribution toward that entire fellowship in His sufferings which Paul saw as the perfection and goal of his spiritual striving.

(3) This rejoicing in suffering seems incomprehensible to modern minds. Christians today are keenly sensitive to all issues of justice, freedom, social equality. The oppression of minorities stirs us to protest; injustice angers us; if we ourselves belong to the persecuted minority, our resentment grows. We expect toleration, protection, freedom, appreciation, even reward.

Curiously, we come to expect also the same generous treatment from God. We anticipate that, whenever we fulfill the supposed conditions, blessing, power, success will automatically follow. Consecration must bring joy; dedicated zeal must produce the intended results; prayer will ensure prosperity, faithful preaching always gathers crowds; sincerity guarantees divine protection. After all, we have our rights!

If we find instead hardship, frustration, sacrifice, we are bewildered, our faith is shaken, we talk of being sadly disillusioned. How far this is from Paul's thinking! He anticipates hardship, weariness, affliction, and finds in them joy. At the very least, he keeps a balanced view of Christian service; the successes and the disappointments, the joys and the regrets, the privileges and the hardships, are alike of God's appointing. But more than this, Paul can rejoice in undeserved suffering when it helps forward Christ's cause, and brings him into closer fellowship with the suffering Christ.

Then, adversity, hardship, disappointment, weariness, and sacrifice take on positive value and spiritual importance. The dream of self-protective security, blessing, and success is seen to be not merely a mirage but a self-impoverishment. There is more to know in Christ than personal happiness, though not many of us can rise to Paul's high viewpoint. But to take up the cross is still the beginning of discipleship, and to carry it faithfully is to walk closely with Christ in the deepest places of His life, and ours.

> I ask not that false calm which many feign,
> And call that peace which is a dearth of pain.
> True calm doth quiver like the calmest star;
> It is that white where all the colours are;
> And for its very vestibule doth own
> The tree of Jesus . . . .
> —STEPHEN PHILLIPS

11

The Church's Cure of Souls
COLOSSIANS 2:1-5

Group therapy is just another name for the healing power of fellowship, but sometimes a new title can make us look again, with new appreciation, at something we have usually taken for granted. Everyone is interested in health, and not least in that balanced health of mind which our tension-strained, fear-haunted, self-analytical generation longs to rediscover. Group therapy suggests psychiatry without its dread, a shared search for mental and moral support, in which individual fears may be submerged in a joint quest with others for total well-being.

Unquestionably, much mental ill health is associated with a lonely, withdrawn isolation from family, friends, and society. Cure must then include reintegration of the individual within some social group, and a genuine sense of belonging with others in a stimulating and supporting circle. In some cases of moral breakdown or addiction, rehabilitation through group ministry may be the only hope left to the soul.

Modern and experimental as all this sounds, the healing power of fellowship is by no means a new discovery. It has been one of the main functions of the church from her earliest days. On the first pages of Scripture we are told that it is not good for man to be alone, and part of God's design for human welfare is to set the lonely within families. The religious *group* is essential to Old Testament religion, and it remains fundamental in the New Testament also.

From the family of God, and the kingdom of Christ, to the disciple band in the Upper Room, the fellowship of believers, the household of faith, and the church which is Christ's body, apostolic emphasis falls upon the Christian community. Prominent among the reasons for this is the Christian's need of his brethren. Luke's picture is of the early church bound together in mutually supporting prayer, encouragement, and benevolence; Paul makes mutual edification one main function of church life—meaning that each Christian circle should be ready to throw around the man or woman under pressure of temptation, persecution, or doubt, and around every new convert, the strong shield of intellectual, moral, emotional, and spiritual support and friendship. To Paul, each local church was a nursery, a school, for saints.

If anything threatened the effectiveness of any church's care and cure of souls, whether it be division and immorality as at Corinth, or controversy as at Galatia, or advent excitement as at Thessalonica, Paul would write urgently and forthrightly a corrective letter. But Colossae, where a strange deceitful philosophy was confusing the church's mind, had been beyond his personal sphere of work, and Paul must therefore justify his concern and intervention. He urges that the Colossians, with all other Gentiles, fall rightly within his apostolic stewardship, and pleads his pastoral responsibility for every church that has not seen his face "that their hearts may be encouraged as they are knit together in love, to have all the riches of assured understanding . . . that no one may delude" them (RSV).

That fourfold summary of pastoral responsibility is also a fourfold description of the church that fulfills its function as a healing fellowship, a school for saints, exercising faithfully the cure of souls.

(1) *Encouragement* is a gracious, rare, and indispensable ministry. It is Christlike, too. How often Jesus moved among people who were downcast, needy, fearful, inarticulate, overawed, always with the heartening "Be of good cheer," or "Be not afraid," and with outstretched hand, ready defense, and open friendship. None was turned

away, repelled, crushed, or made to feel insignificant. In His presence men and women grew taller, hope was kindled, the smoking flax was never quenched nor the bruised reed broken. At His word, things long despaired of seemed possible again.

Encouragement is apostolic, as well as Christlike. Barnabas was given by his colleagues the lovely nickname, "son of encouragement," and so he stands in Christian history, first of many whose chief claim to Christian gratitude lies with the weak souls they made strong, the small people they made great. Generous mind, generous hand, and generous heart combined in Barnabas to make a model for Bunyan's Mr. Great-heart, whose task appointed by the King was to go before pilgrims on the Royal Highway with sword and shield, to guide and defend, to call to the weakest to stand nearest to him in danger, and through all perils and temptations to bring every pilgrim safely to the verge of Jordan.

Not all pastors are such ministers of encouragement. It is easier to be a perfectionist, and expect others to be the same; sometimes it relieves one's own conscience to criticize, to scold, and to condemn. Not all churches are fellowships of encouragement: a forbidding, reserved, censorious, or critical atmosphere soon makes the stumbling convert, the ignorant inquirer, the struggling backslider, acutely aware that he is not welcome, or understood, or wanted.

But such un-Christlike ministries, such unapostolic churches, will know nothing of the cure of souls. A healing fellowship demands the gift of tireless Christian comfort—that "lifts the drooping hands, strengthens the feeble knees, makes straight paths of shining example that what is lame may not be put out of joint but rather be healed" (*see* Hebrews 12:12, 13).

(2) The *unity* of Christians "knit together in love" is no small part of the cure of souls. It is in the loyalty of a Christian fellowship that the lonely, beset soul finds its greatest human support. Continual reconciliation is an essential part of every pastoral ministry, and every true church is a group where many opposites combine, where people of many varying backgrounds, levels of culture, degrees of status and of talent, find unity in Christ.

True, the natural differences that tend to set people apart are too often reinforced by widely varying spiritual experiences, each claimed to be the true experience of God; by widely different religious opinions, each asserted to be the whole truth of the gospel. Such difference and variety can deepen into distrust and division that sets even Christians one against another. But where this happens, the gospel itself is being denied and one primary function of the church is being destroyed.

One of the oldest names for *priest* means *bridge builder*. No aspect of Christian ministry could be more relevant. The church's leader, and the whole fellowship, can do nothing more urgently necessary than to help people understand themselves, understand each other, understand the things that divide and embitter, and lead them from indifference, or alienation, into fruitful partnership. To build bridges between old and young, between parent and child, between races, between classes and sections of society, between Christian and non-Christian, between estranged husband and wife, is never easy. Mere toleration at a distance, peace without understanding, a dutiful charity without real interest, or any spark of compassion, will not do. Christian unity is a slower, deeper process.

Gently to heal the hurt of years, sympathetically to melt the resentments that engender the unforgiving spirit, courageously to lead men to the truth about themselves, in love and with positive purpose, shrewdly to perceive the real issue within some poisoned relationship and bring it firmly into daylight, resolutely to bend proud people to self-understanding, penitence, and apology—such a ministry is the task of a fellowship made strong in its own assurance of the forgiveness of God. Only within such an atmosphere of moral understanding, under such a searchlight of genuine unity of purpose, can souls estranged from others and bereft of love and friendship find themselves again "knit together in love." That is a cure of souls which can be achieved *only* by healing fellowship.

(3) Yet precious though encouragement and friendship are to souls in trouble, no problem of the spiritual life is finally solved without *understanding,* illumination, and new direction. "Nothing is ever settled" says an experienced sage, "until it is settled right." But to see and follow the right, in any complicated situation, needs "the full assurance of understanding." The cure of souls must therefore include some care for their Christian education, their growth in grace and in the knowledge of Christ.

This was especially needed, of course, at Colossae, where strange new teaching bewildered Christian minds and undermined Christian confidence just when clarity and strong conviction were essential. That is why Paul had prayed for the Colossians greater wisdom and understanding; why he has already recalled the need for sound learning if daily behavior is to be consistent and wise. Now he longs that they may have also, not mere repetition of the first principles of the doctrine of Christ, but all the riches of assured understanding and the knowledge of God's mystery, of Christ, in whom are hid all the treasures of wisdom and knowledge.

Understanding, wisdom, knowledge: the terms are intellectual, but the result is spiritual enrichment, the "riches," the "treasures" of Christ being explored and experienced and enjoyed by the growing faith of maturing believers. This is no mere information, such as can be obtained from pamphlets and paperbacks and lesson notes. It concerns insight, and the knowledge of God, a firm grasp of the "open secret" of Christ, and an understanding of the rich experience garnered in the living church. Only so are Christians armed against the pressures of society, the denials of the sceptic, the cynicism of the conscienceless, the betrayals of the disloyal, the sophistries of the tempter. A church truly concerned about the growth, the health, and the safety of its converts and its children will take great care that they are taught the faith and made to share the deep things of God.

(4) The least expected, and most difficult, element in the cure of souls is *protection*. Because there are those "who would delude with beguiling speech," Paul would shield the Colossian Christians from all danger. He cannot stand aloof, leaving converts to find their own way, run their own risks, solve their own problems. Each Christian leader inherits not only the pastoral ideal of the shepherd caring for the sheep, but also the prophets' ideal of the watchman set over the city to care for the safety of God's people.

He that winneth souls is wise: he that keepeth them in the King's Highway may need to be wiser still. Pastoral protectiveness must know where to stop. Mature Christians must make their own decisions, exercise their own faith. But even earnest people can make mistakes for lack of a timely word of counsel; weak people can fall by the way for want of a faithful word of warning. Overzealous people can blunder because no one had courage to take them aside and tactfully advise restraint. How faithfully Jesus dealt with the fears, the misunderstandings, the weak faith, of Peter, and Thomas, and Philip! And most of us have at some time owed our safety to strong people who stood between us and the enemy, who spoke the difficult warning, the necessary rebuke, and who stretched a steadying arm to save us from the abyss.

True care for souls is plainly manifold and demanding. Almost accidentally Paul lets fall his secret: "I want you to know how greatly I strive for you . . . . Though absent in body, yet I am with you in spirit, rejoicing to see your good order and the firmness of your faith in Christ." That means more than "I have been thinking about you, wishing I were with you." It means a sympathetic and imaginative identification with those unknown Christians so many miles away across mountain and valley. Once he had spoken similarly to the church at Corinth, but there he promised that his spirit would be among them as they met for a solemn act of judgment against a moral offender. To the Colossians he can speak of being so near to them that he shares their joy and the firmness of their faith.

"Who is weak, and I am not weak? who is disgraced, and I burn not?" (*see* 2 Corinthians 11:29). Such imaginative, emotional identification with others is the heart of all care for souls. We need not ask where Paul learned it: it is the central principle of our salvation— "He was numbered with the transgressors . . . made sin for us . . . was not ashamed to call us brethren." We are saved, redeemed, have forgiveness and peace, only because He so cared, so identified Himself with us. We can care for men only in His name, and in His way.

12

What More Can You Possibly Want?
COLOSSIANS 2:6, 7

There is great art in knowing when to come to the point. The advertiser will go a long way round to engage attention, kindle curiosity, insinuate information, before he reveals that he merely wants you to buy. The child soon learns to do the same. "Mommy, you know Kathleen who lives along the road? Well, she told me that when her cousin Joan was on vacation with them, and was playing with a ball in the house where they were staying, she broke a window, and she was so frightened, but nothing happened; everybody just laughed, and no one was cross at all. She was lucky, wasn't she? Mommy, what makes people lucky, like that?" Mommy carelessly

says, "I do not know—why do you ask?" To which comes the
disarming reply, "Well, Mommy, I've just dropped a cup."

It is something every woman knows. And every good preacher:
when to come to the point, and when to postpone it, and prepare
for it. Paul comes to his point plainly and sharply: "As therefore
you received Christ Jesus the Lord, so live in him, rooted and built
up in him and established in the faith, just as you were taught,
abounding in thanksgiving" (RSV). But because the point is sharp,
and he is a stranger to his readers, he has prepared well for it.
He leads up to it with warm greeting, complimentary thanksgiving,
glowing report, nice commendation of their minister. His prayer for
their enlightenment had led him to a wonderful exposition of the
greatness of Christ, touching closely the strange ideas abroad in
Colossae—but he had not implied that anyone there had succumbed
to that teaching. And he had summarized their spiritual experience
as sure, deep, and significant. Even after all that, Paul has not yet
said why he is writing to them at all.

Instead, he pauses to explain his deep pastoral interest in this
church he did not found. Only then does he venture this firm and
forthright appeal—"As therefore you received Christ . . . so live in
him, rooted . . . built up . . . established . . . just as you were
taught." The new philosophy being marketed at Colossae made large
claims and offered large promises: greater wisdom, marvelous divine
secrets, deeper spiritual satisfaction were available if men would
worship angel beings, avoid certain foods, accept the hidden, occult
mysteries about the universe which visions or advanced intellectual
doctrines could impart. It offered a so-called higher version of
Christianity for the elite, the highbrows, the spiritually superior—and
few fools can resist that sort of snob appeal.

So some were tempted, became critical of the church, sceptical
of the simple gospel, dissatisfied with their present level of spiritual
experience, and they played with heresies—as so many modern
Christians do, chasing after any new sect, or cult, or strange medley
of religious ideas that calls itself a new revelation, listening avidly
to any slick doorstep salesman of ancient heresies long exploded—
because their Christian lives are superficial, unsatisfying, disappointing.

The surest, safest preventative against all sub-Christian deviations
is a full experience of the fullness of Christ. What dissatisfied
Christians think to discover in the various extreme and tangential
sects, exists already for them in the gospel they have received, if

only they had been properly instructed, and led to comprehend the length and breadth, the height and depth, of Christian salvation. The sure antidote to all the misrepresentations, exaggerations, and perversions of the gospel that clutter Christendom, is to be "rooted . . . built up . . . established . . ." in Christ, just as you were taught.

That is Paul's point. "What more do you want than you already have in Christ?" He is the firstborn of all creation, the firstborn from the dead, the beloved Son and King and the Redeemer; in Him dwells all the fullness of the Godhead bodily, all the treasures of wisdom and knowledge. What can any other teacher, or doctrine, or ritual offer that Jesus has not already procured for us? Stand fast on what you know; explore the faith you have; grasp to the full all that there is in Christ for you, and you will find all you need of wisdom, challenge, ideals, hope, power, and blessing.

> Thou, O Christ, art all I want,
> More than all in Thee I find . . . .

that is why this text is the pith and focus of the whole letter to Colossae: "As you received Christ Jesus, so live in Him . . . rooted . . . built up . . . established . . . just as you were taught."

Paul looks back, you will notice, to something that has happened in the past; and then he urges something for the present because of what happened in the past.

What happened in the past was this, you received Christ Jesus the Lord, just as you were taught.

Paul has already recalled how wonderfully these Colossians responded to the gospel. There had been great times in Colossae; many lives were changed, the gospel bore fruit. Later Paul will remind them gently what kind of people they had been to contrast that with the kind of people they are, and still can be, now. Out of a dark and superstitious paganism full of fear, they had been translated into a kingdom of light and love and joy. That total life transformation turned upon two simple events.

(1) On the one hand was something they had been taught. Epaphras, a good man, had brought from Ephesus news which had spread from Jerusalem, from Galilee, from Bethlehem. The news implied a message, a teaching, a pattern of thought and of living, and it broke upon them with conviction and promise and great power. And not

least, the life and changed quality of the teacher, of Epaphras, whom they knew, gave added weight to the teaching.

That is how the good news comes to all of us: an exciting, revolutionary, illuminating reinterpretation of all we have ever known or thought or felt, stemming from the story of the Babe, the Boy, the Man upon a cross and in a garden. And it comes framed with reverence and affection in the lives we most admire, of parents, teachers, friends, and pastors, who led our earliest steps toward Christ. Remember, says Paul, how you were taught, and do not be disloyal—do not let down those who were among the best people you have known.

(2) On the other hand was something they had received. We cannot forever believe just because we are told. The time comes when what others say becomes our own: "We received Christ Jesus the Lord." The message has for us the ring of truth; our lives are changed, our sins forgiven, our homes are different, our thoughts are cleansed, our hearts rejoice. What had been news with a promise becomes a conviction built upon experience. Like the Samaritans of old, we cease to be Christians by hearsay or inheritance, and make our personal discovery: we believe, not because of someone else's word, but because we have seen Him for ourselves.

For this too happens to all of us. The truth handed down mediates a discovery of our own; others tell the message, bear their testimony, and suddenly it is not flesh and blood that reveals the meaning but the Father in heaven. Truth taught becomes truth confirmed. This, Paul insists, *has happened*. It is right to recall the beginning of Christian life for us, lest we too go wandering away, seeking what in fact we already possess. "Be true to your teachers! Be true to your own experience! What more can you possibly want?"

What Paul urges for the present, because of what happened in the past, is equally clear: "As you received . . . so live . . . rooted . . . built up . . . established." In other words, "Stay put!"

That is scarcely advice which we restless, go-getting, unsettled modern people ever want to hear. We hate standing fast: we prefer running around even if it gets us nowhere. We are history's inveterate mobiles, caravanners, rootless, of no fixed abode. Yet see how perceptive, and apt, Paul's counsel is, after all. For he puts it in four different, significant ways.

(1) "Be established" suggests the need to get some things settled, if life is to be consistent, strong, and purposeful. It means taking your bearings, getting a grip on things, deciding where you are and where you are going. A man cannot live all his life in soft sand, blown about by every wind, feeding his mind only upon questions, never upon answers. Paul's word is a legal term for guaranteeing, or confirming, something settled and signed—and there are some things a man has to put his name to, in the end. Youth may be flexible, undirected, unpredictable because unreliable; but maturity demands some fixed points—indeed, maturity *means* getting basic things clear, the direction set, becoming, not a member of the establishment but something infinitely better, an established person in your own right.

This kind of firmness and consistency involves laying down the main lines of your belief about life, the main lines of your character, the main lines of your career. Christians do this by accepting Christ as Teacher, Example, and Lord. He becomes the blueprint, the ground plan, of the house of life—and many remain spiritually unsatisfied, mentally and morally at sixes and sevens, just because they never got the ground plan of their lives established, once for all.

(2) Yet a ground plan is not yet a home. Be built up, says Paul. Build on the blueprint—do not frame it with admiration when your life has no walls on which to hang it! Let the house of life rise steadily from the footings, foursquare, course upon course as the days and weeks pass into years, until the depth of undeniable experience and the firmness of fine habit grown strong with use provide a storm-proof home for the aging soul.

Paul is fond of this figure of speech: he talks frequently about Christians being built up, edified, as though the Christian life rises like some colossal temple, buttressed by faith and hope and love, and indwelt by the Spirit of the Christian's Lord. Perhaps originally he learned it from Christ: ". . . whosoever heareth these sayings of mine, and doeth them, [is like a man] which built his house upon a rock . . ." (Matthew 7:24).

"And doeth them . . . ." That is being built up: character, and principle, and conscience, and deliberate Christian action; habit and attitude and work and service; home and marriage and friendship and parenthood and worship—building life on the ground plan of the gospel. Some remain unsatisfied, spiritually homeless and unsheltered, because they never built upon the faith they once professed.

(3) Appropriately enough, Paul seems to add "live in Him"—dwell in the house you have built in Christ. But his word means something intensely practical and ethical: conduct your daily life in Christ— literally, walk the world in Christ, clothed with Him, in all you do and are and say, letting men see your Lord. Before he is through, Paul will show how this affects life at home, at work, in society, in church, among friends, and on the street. Here he reminds in a word that the unsatisfied Christian is often one who has never worked his faith into the warp and woof of everyday life and action, never let it out of Sunday into the week, never let it out of his heart into his days. For piety confined to worship, prayer, and inward feeling, invariably turns sour, and disappoints the soul.

(4) Yet for all this, settling the plan, building the house, walking daily in Christ, do not spell stagnation. We are to be rooted in Christ, also. The building is fixed and steadfast, in a static way; the tree is also fixed, and steadfast, but in a growing way, sending its roots farther down, its branches out and up, increasing, swelling, casting a wider shade, bearing increasing fruit, as the years pass.

That is what this letter is written to say, above all else: you have a great Christ, an eternal, divine, exhaustless Saviour, in whom is all the Godhead, all the treasure the heart can need. *Get rooted deep in Him;* draw from Him all your heart can crave; explore His fullness—and you shall be full, ever renewed, and ever fruitful. Twice the figure occurs in the Old Testament—the tree planted by rivers of living water: Jeremiah says the man of faith is like that tree— evergreen, never wilting, never dying; the Psalmist says the man who meditates in the Word of God is like that—bearing his fruit in his season, and his leaf does not wither. Paul is saying that the man rooted in Christ is like that too—satisfied, nourished, rooted securely and reaching ever upwards at the same time!

What more can you possibly want?

"In Him the Fullness"

13

And You Are Filled
COLOSSIANS 2:8-10

Every area of discussion has its jargon, which we are apt to despise as the substitute for thought. But sometimes subtle changes in the current terminology of a subject can express new insights and progress in understanding. For some time now, people who have failed to fit into the social pattern, refusing to conform to the accepted norms of behavior, have been categorized as delinquent, rebellious, misfits, crazy-mixed-up, or just "lost." Each word has its assumption, its nuance, its diagnosis. But a new term has crept into social concern, and has rapidly established itself.

The head of an American rehabilitation center for alcoholics, drug addicts, nonintegrates and drop-outs was discussing the needs and methods of his work: for his varied patients he used most often the generalized, but compassionate, term *inadequates*—suggesting people without resource, unequipped for life, needing support. A British telephone service offering personal help to students, whether lonely and needing friends, in trouble and needing rescue, bewildered and needing counsel, or "hooked" and needing a "fix," described its many clients by the same general term—"inadequate, needing support."

In a personal conversation, a young woman university graduate, cultured and aware, confessed that she was under immense stress, confused, her life plan at a dead end: despairingly she blurted out "I just cannot cope!" This is something deeper and more serious than delinquency and rebelliousness: it is the sad admission of mental, moral, and nervous inadequacy for living. It is the self-exposure of an empty soul.

Behind this spiritual malaise, most probably, the old human and humbling sense of creatureliness and mortality is asserting itself, and finds no answering, reassuring faith. The result is a consciousness of inescapable limitations; of being utterly dependent without having anything to depend upon; of having far greater obligations than re-

81

sources. Personality is left drained, exhausted, and discovers no means
of infilling and renewal—sometimes in spite of many attempts and
continual disappointment with proffered "secrets," cults, creeds, and
experiences. As Jeremiah said long ago of his baffled, frustrated, exhausted generation, ". .   my people . . . have forsaken me the
fountain of living waters, and hewed them out cisterns, broken cisterns, that can hold no water" (Jeremiah 2:13).

This was the trouble, in part, at Colossae. The new and strange
doctrines, rituals, and regulations disturbing Christians there would
have had no attraction for hearts full and overflowing with Christian
joy. Many were dissatisfied, spiritually hungry, wistful, eager for a
greater experience of blessing. It was the promise of more wonderful
visions, deeper secrets, fuller knowledge, that made the new teaching
persuasive. Paul expects a man's religious faith to enrich, and liberate,
and infill his life: he warns expressly against the specious philosophy
that threatens to rob them of their "treasures" in Christ.

The new teaching was an "empty deceit" based on human tradition, inspired by the spirits of this world and not by Christ. And it
was predatory: so far from enriching it impoverished; it was unprofit-
able as well as untrue. He warns, "It will make prey of you," treat
you as spoil, and plunder your hearts, leaving you less adequate than
ever for the demands and afflictions of life. Why let anything do this
to you—when in Christ dwells all the fullness—and *you are full* in
Him?

That is Paul's answer to every inadequate, dissatisfied, disappointed, disillusioned, and exhausted soul.

In Christ is all the fullness—Paul has said this three times in thirty-
eight verses. All the fullness of God was pleased to dwell in Him; in
Him are all the treasures of wisdom and knowledge; in Him the whole
fullness of deity dwells bodily. Paul has spelled out his meaning, too,
in tremendous affirmations about the preeminence of Christ in creation, in relation to God, in the universe at large, in the experience
of the church, and in the life of the Christian. And to emphasize still
further these great declarations of the fullness of Christ, he has directed them accurately and relentlessly against the false ideas current
in Colossae.

The new teachers held that Christ was the lowest link in a long
chain of mediators between God and man: Paul replies that in Him
dwells all the fullness of deity itself. The new teachers held that an
infinite number of spiritual beings of various kinds—thrones, domin-

ions, principalities, authorities—filled the void between earth and heaven, and so were called "the fullness": Paul answers forthrightly that in Him all the fullness was pleased to dwell. The new teachers offered to those capable of intellectual understanding a new revelation of "advanced" Christian knowledge, divine secrets, sacred mysteries, and the like: Paul declares that in Christ are hid all the treasures of wisdom and knowledge.

Nor is it only one apostle, facing one local situation, who so insists upon the fullness of Christ. John says it too, in his characteristic way. ". . . the Word was made flesh, and dwelt among us . . . full of grace and truth . . . . And of his fulness have we all received, and grace for grace" (John 1:14-16). From His fullness: it is one of John's great themes; fullness of grace, fullness of truth, fullness or abundance of life, fullness of joy—all made available in Christ for thirsty, exhausted, inadequate men. Sometimes, following Jesus, he pictures it as a well deep and never running dry, so that he who drinks of it shall never thirst again; sometimes as a flowing river, renewing, fertilizing, refreshing the society in which the Christian moves, so that from him who believes in Christ shall flow rivers of living water.

That is the practical importance of a right view of Christ and of His divine glory. We affirm that He is rich, that we in our poverty might find riches. We declare His divinity, because it is in His divinity we find our only hope for helpless, inadequate humanity. Paul contends, and we contend, for the fullness of Christ, because only as He is filled with the grace, the power, the truth, the life of God can He meet the desperate need of bankrupt souls—as we know He does.

> He is a path, if any be misled;
> He is a robe, if any naked be;
> If any chance to hunger, he is bread;
> If any be a bondman, he is free;
> If any be but weak, how strong is he!
> To dead men life he is, to sick men health,
> To blind men sight, and to the needy, wealth;
> A pleasure without loss, a treasure without stealth.
> —GILES FLETCHER, JR.

In Christ is *all* the fullness.

And you are full in Him. Listen to John again: "As the living Father hath sent me, and I live by the Father: so he that eateth me, even he shall live by me" (John 6:57). The living Father: one thinks of God the Father as, so to speak, a great reservoir, a mighty illimitable ocean, of goodness and truth and power and love, overflowing in mercy and plenteous in redemption. *I live by the Father*: one thinks of Christ, the channel of all that God wishes to give, brimful of grace, conveying that divine fullness into human history, expressing God's truth, enshrining God's power, mediating God's love, into human experience. *He who feeds on me shall live by Me:* one thinks of the Christian, linked through the channel of Christ with all the fullness that is in God, drinking, receiving, filled and overflowing, becoming in turn a channel to a thirsty world.

So John's gospel: but that is Paul's meaning, too. In Him is the fullness, and you are filled full in Him. The rest of this challenging epistle works out that great theme. Of course we are not filled with the fullness of deity: that is His alone. But we can be filled with everything the human heart can need, or can contain, or can possess. Do you complain of poverty of spiritual experience, a restless, unsatisfied searching for something more? Paul's answer is, there *is* nothing more than you possess in Christ.

In Him are hid all the treasures of wisdom and knowledge—sufficient for the Christian mind. *Christ is our life*—sufficient for the Christian heart. *He is preeminent in all things*—sufficient for Christian devotion. *Put on the Lord Jesus Christ*—sufficient for the Christian goal. *Set your affection on things above, where Christ is*—sufficient for all Christian aspiration. *Christ is seated on the right hand of God*—sufficient for all Christian courage. *Christ, who is our life, shall appear*—sufficient for the Christian hope. The wonderful fullness of Christ spells a wonderful fullness of Christian experience for all who will. Paul covets that for us all.

We have no need, as the Colossians had none, to go searching for fuller life, deeper knowledge, more exciting experience. So many new cults and "-ologies" and "-isms" promise so much and provide so little. They leave the unsatisfied heart further impoverished, disappointed, tending toward cynicism and unbelief. We do not need another Christ—nor a substitute for Christ—but a better understanding of the Christ we know. Faith laying hold of the fullness of Christ finds fullness of life—that is the only answer to low-temperature, low-level, low-voltage Christian discipleship.

But it is the answer too for all who find life too exacting, too demanding, too exhausting. For all who feel inadequate, unable to cope,

at the end of their resources—this is the gospel: in Christ is all fullness, and you can come to fullness of life in Him.

> I heard the voice of Jesus say,
> "Behold, I freely give
> The living water—thirsty one,
> Stoop down, and drink, and live."
> I came to Jesus and I drank
> Of that life-giving stream;
> My thirst was quenched, my soul revived,
> And now I live in Him.
>
> —HORATIUS BONAR

14

What Christ Has Done
COLOSSIANS 2:11-15

Every happily married man considers that the sort of woman he chose
is the only sort of woman any sensible man would choose. Every
dedicated sportsman thinks that the way he plays the game is the
only way it should be played. Every earnest preacher believes that
his way of preaching the everlasting gospel is the best way of all. And
every rejoicing Christian is sure that what Christ has done for him,
and means to him, is the true heart of the gospel—all else is relatively
unimportant.

It is natural all should think so. Yet maturing of mind and widening
of experience largely consist in coming to share the happiness of other
sorts of people, to admire the skill, appreciate the methods, rejoice
in the spiritual experience, that is different from our own. So we
develop sympathy, insight, a larger experience for ourselves, and
often make quite unforeseen discoveries. Another's unusual testimony
may often reveal our own unsuspected limitations of faith.

If we were asked, simply and suddenly, what Christ has done for
us, we should probably name one or two particular ways in which
Christ came to mean everything to our hearts. Ask Paul, and he

names six! When he would recall the Colossian Christians from wandering among idle speculations and specious promises of new religious excitements, he lists six things Christ has already done for them—six things they have already seen and experienced and known.

Three things the Lord has done for us concern the inner experience of the soul—its safety, its liberty, its victory. The other three things the Lord has done have to do with the wider field of God's relationship with man, the new status and position into which Christ brings all who believe on Him. If long words might be permitted, we might speak of the subjective side of Christ's work—what He does within ourselves—and the objective side of His work—what He does for us before God, and Himself, and eternity.

Paul begins with that wider, objective work of Christ for us.

(1) Christ has, he says, made us alive to God. As Gentiles, and as sinners, the Colossians had been "twice dead": dead in trespasses and sins, with the death that is the inevitable wages of sin; and also dead in the darkness of paganism, idolatry, and ignorance. But they had been "made alive." The coming of the gospel had been like the breath of the divine wind in Ezekiel's valley of dry bones.

Out of the places of death had come a stirring of life and renewal, of resurrection and hope. Men had been quickened with Christ, raised with Christ, made to sit together in heavenly places with Christ. They had felt the pulse of new strength, new awareness, new desire and eagerness, new energy and joy. Christ had called the Colossians out of the valley of shadows into His glorious light, out of the Lazarus-tomb of sin and the winding-sheets of ignorance and idolatry, into the daylight of life eternal. This they had known: whereas they were dead, now they are alive with Christ, alive in Christ to God—awake to God, aware of God, responding to God, experiencing the love of God. For Christ has given them life.

(2) And Christ has, Paul says, brought you into living relation also with Himself. Incredibly, you have been made one with the divine Messiah-Saviour. The dramatic events of His own life have been re-enacted in us—we have been allowed to share the central redemptive acts that achieve salvation! "You were buried with him in baptism, in which you were also raised with him through faith in the working of God, who raised him from the dead" (RSV).

It is vivid and dramatic enough to speak of the beginning of Chris-

tian life as a "conversion" or turning round to face a new direction;
as a "new birth"—the miracle of a new beginning at any age; or as
a "new creation"—suggesting that not only the man himself but all
his world has been made over in Christ. But to speak of that Christian
beginning as a "death and resurrection with Christ" is yet more
startling. All these expressions describe the gift of new life from God
realized through repentance and faith, and each has its own important
shade of meaning. To say that Christian life begins as I come into
union with Christ, the dying-rising Saviour—a union so close and
personal that I too die to sin and rise with Him to new life—is to
make me realize that conversion is not only glad and wonderful—it
is sheer miracle.

Paul evidently expects the Colossians to be familiar with this language, and aware of this experience. Christ had so united them to
Himself; they had indeed died to sin and the old Christless life; they
had risen again to victorious, new, and endless life in Him. Henceforth, all their experience, their purpose, their work, their progress,
and their hope centered upon their new relationship to Him. That
made them what they were. And that too, Christ had done.

(3) And Christ, Paul says, has done yet a third thing for us: He
has given us a place among the people of God. The Colossian church
was mainly Gentile in character. Those who were Jews among them
would feel, as Paul did, the immense, inexpressible privilege of belonging to the people whom God had called into being, cherished
through the centuries, shaped for His own purposes in history, and
called His own. The symbol and badge of that privileged election was
the rite of circumcision, and with immeasurable generosity of mind
and heart Paul embraces within the chosen people these Christian
Gentiles at Colossae and declares that Christ has given to them, too,
the badge of the Covenant.

Usually Paul insists that the outward symbol is nothing: here he
goes further. The Colossians, he says, have all the symbol they need
—the inward mark of Christ, made without hands. They are already
the people of God, holy and beloved, chosen and commissioned for
God's work. They are no more strangers, aliens, far off; they have
been received into the commonwealth of Israel, the household of faith.
Christ has done this, again: He has set us within the current of God's
purpose in history; He has placed us within the Covenant that gov-
erns God's ways with men; He has given us a place within the divine

community, the Israel of God. We are God's people—and earth knows no greater privilege.

So much has the Lord done for us, in relation to God, to Himself, and to God's people. But He has done more yet.

Paul turns to that more intimate, subjective work of Christ within us. It could be summed up, essentially, in one word: freedom.

(1) For Christ had set them free from the past, with the freedom we call forgiveness. Indeed, Paul suddenly turns from "you" to "we" in order to include his own wonderful experience of pardon: "having forgiven us all our trespasses" (RSV). The memory that he had persecuted the church never wholly left the apostle; it seemed to him that God had chosen to make him an exhibition, as ". . . the foremost of sinners . . ." toward whom the grace of the Lord overflowed that ". . . in me, as the foremost, Jesus Christ might display his perfect patience for an example to those who were to believe . . ." (1 Timothy 1:15, 16 RSV).

Yet though the memory never died, the past was forgiven: Paul was free of its guilt and power. The Colossians had known this pardoning release, too. Paul chooses a word with the special flavor of being received, undeservedly, into great favor—the word Luke uses in the parable of the two debtors, where the lord of the house "frankly forgave them both" with the utmost favor and generosity. Only he who has gone in fear of meeting his deserts knows what it means to be forgiven; only he who has borne through the years the heavy burden of his sins knows what it means to feel the straps snap, the burden slip and roll into the tomb of the crucified—and break into John Bunyan's song,

> Blest cross! blest Sepulchre! blest rather be
> The Man that there was put to shame for me.

"To a man doomed to die, pardon is life," says Agar Beet. The Colossians knew how true that is. This again the Lord had done for them, as He has done for us.

(2) The same Lord had set them inwardly free from the burden of legalist obligations. He had ". . . canceled the bond which stood against us with its legal demands; this he set aside, nailing it to the cross" (RSV). It does not much matter whether Paul is thinking of a document—an IOU—recording the unpaid debt, as in the parable

of the unjust steward; or of a document registering the accusations of the law against us, as with the "title" set above Jesus on the cross. Paul's meaning is plain. All demands and accusations are at an end; the bond preserving them is obliterated, and publicly displayed as settled!

Our fears are past, and with them all slavery to the law has been cancelled. We live no longer by outward regulations but by inward and willing constraint: we are free to be the kind of men that Christ has made us *want* to be. Paul speaks with deep feeling: the law's documented demands are first washed from the parchment altogether; then the document is set aside, out of the way; and then the cancellation is published to all by the nailing of the blank record to Christ's cross. Paul is emphatic, not only because some are seeking to reimpose Jewish legalism upon the church at Colossae, but because of his own bitter memories of that futile bondage to written commandments which are "against us," which "awaken sin," the "letter which kills." Paul had reason to know that the law could not save.

"Stand fast therefore in the liberty wherewith Christ has made you free," Paul pleads elsewhere, "let no one entangle you again with any yoke of bondage" (*see* Galatians 5:1). You are free, he says here, "why then be subject to rules and regulations?" For spiritual freedom is the second of Christ's inward gifts.

(3) The third is, freedom from the demonic powers of the world. More real, and terrifying, than any Jewish legalism, for the Colossian Christians, was the potent, ubiquitous, immeasurable menace of the spirit world, a dread of which we today can have little understanding, and no imagination. Several million evil spirits, "the elemental spirits of the universe" (Galatians 4:3 RSV), were believed to beset man at every turn of his daily life, producing in individuals and in society all kinds of disease, madness, evil, violence, and vice.

Ranged in a hierarchy of ascending powers, evil forces opposed all good, and wrought man's undoing by stealth, by strength, and by demonic magic. Against them men were pathetically helpless, despite innumerable protective charms, rituals, and secrets. The spirit world was no mere morbidity of mind, but a terror presenting to early Christianity its major challenge, at least in the gentile world. Already in this letter Paul has insisted that whatever powers there be, Christ created them, and is their Head, and will reconcile all to God. Believers have been delivered from the power of darkness into the kingdom of Christ's love. Now he goes further: Christ has triumphed over all such powers, disarming them, making a public example of them, triumphing over them.

This was the gospel's answer to the dread of demon powers: the ruler of this world has no power over Christ; he is cast out; the Stronger than he has bound him and plundered his goods; God raised Christ from the dead, and set Him at His own right hand in heavenly places far above all principality and power and every name that is named. And God has raised you there with Him—Christ leads us in the train of His triumph. The New Testament does not deny the spirit powers: it declares them defeated—so we need not fear them any longer. They are nothing to us—we are set free by the supreme victory of Christ.

So from all forms of inner bondage Christ has made us free—from sin, and law, and fear. Sin binds all men; legalism and demonism were the strangely assorted threats being promulgated at Colossae. But Christ has broken all our bonds, settled all our debts, and conquered all our foes—at one stroke! This, too, the Lord has done: He confers safety, liberty, and victory, through His cross.

All this is the Lord's doing, and it is marvelous in our eyes. A new relationship to God, to Christ Himself, and to God's people; a new experience of forgiveness, of freedom, and of triumph—what can any other message or cult or ritual or philosophy do for us, more than Christ has done? Remember what He has already done, and know that He can still do more than we ask, or think.

(*Note:* A number of highly debatable judgments underlie this exposition; for discussion of other views, commentaries should be consulted.)

15

Substance—Not Shadows
COLOSSIANS 2:16-23

The ancient fable of the dog carrying a bone, pausing at its own reflection in the water and grabbing at the mirrored prize only to lose the one it had, embodies a warning old as human thought, yet never outgrown. Men are but shadows chasing shadows and often like to have it so. When reality appalls, shadows may comfort, or at least distract.

Even in religion. There are intellectual shadows, doctrinal theories and opinions that mean little and matter less, but keep the mind from serious truth. There are emotional shadows, religious excitements, and intensely morbid, or ecstatic "soul feelings" which neither prove nor produce anything good, but pass for spirituality. There are mystic shadows, voices, visions, dreams, and private revelations mistaken for a living faith. And ritual shadows, that set approved patterns of words properly pronounced and prescribed actions meticulously performed, above daily trust, obedience, and duty.

Of course, right doctrine, deep feeling, the inward perception of truth and the outward reverence of worship, all have true place within religion: but pursued, either for its own sake, they all become shadows of the great reality—a personal experience of God. The story of the church is littered with examples of well-meaning folk who enthusiastically chased shadows and missed the solid truth.

It was happening at Colossae.

Some there were pursuing the shade of so-called "philosophy and empty deceit, according to human tradition . . . and not according to Christ . . . an appearance of wisdom" (RSV). "Advanced ideas for advanced intellectual Christians" were being peddled in preference to the faith they had been taught. The source seems to have been a widespread fashion of Greek thought, which by insisting that the pure God could have no possible relationship with evil matter, denied the creation of the world by God, and the incarnation of the Son in human flesh. Between the pure Spirit and evil matter, it was alleged, stretched an interminable chain of beings of gradually descending spirituality, of which Jesus was but the last and lowest link, just above man.

Imprisoned man's only hope lay in liberation through enlightenment, possible only to the intellectually gifted and well-taught. Paul had little patience with this salvation only for the educationally elite —he boasted a gospel for every man. He had still less patience with the speculative thought-spinning of men intoxicated with their own intellectual cleverness. For him, the word of truth was a gospel which bore fruit in the whole world; the only wisdom that matters is that which leads to a life worthy of the Lord, pleasing, fruitful, and growing in the understanding of God.

For Paul, all the treasures of wisdom and knowledge are laid up for us in Christ. Beside that enriching, fruitful, energizing, satisfying knowledge of the truth, all "vain philosophy" is but intellectual shadows, empty because without solidity or substance; a mere human tradition because without authority or significance. To his mind, truth is something that one lives by, not something to fool yourself with. And the truth men could live well by was—the truth of Christ.

But some at Colossae were chasing other shadows: the ritual regulations that control food and drink, attendance at festivals, seasonal observances, holy Sabbaths. These are the external prescriptions of religion, the conventional evidences of piety. Mere human precepts, says Paul: all negative, as though religion consists in *not* doing things; all trivial, too, for they concern what perishes at a touch. Why submit to this idle imposition of needless obligations? And why, above all, let people sit in judgment upon you in such matters?

Such is the force of habit, the numbing effect of familiarity, that any expression of Christian truth, or loyalty, or worship, can become mere formality, an empty and powerless ritual. At times when the spiritual life burns low, familiar patterns of worship, belief, and prayer can be our strength and bring renewal. At least as often, they can become the shadow of what once they stood for, and take the place of real faith, dedication, and fellowship with God. Then the form of godliness has insulated us against its power: the outward symbols of discipleship have become more important than inward love to Christ.

It may be well occasionally to change the patterns of our response to Christ, lest any good custom should corrupt the soul. It might even be a means of grace to be deprived, sometimes, of the usual avenues of worship, that we may find again the Substance when the shadows are denied. Prophets and reformers have had so often to inveigh against the too familiar forms, the overelaborate ritual, that hides God from us. Not our sins alone, but insincere pieties, can separate us from Him with whom we have to do.

> Not for our sins alone
>   Thy mercy, Lord, we sue;
> Let fall Thy pitying glance
>   On our devotions too,
> What we have done for Thee,
> And what we think to do.
>   —HENRY TWELLS

Paul has in mind also the emotional shadows which some chase: the excitements and ecstasies kindled by visions and voices and intense "spiritual experiences" beloved of the introspective. He speaks sharply of those who take their stand on visions, who claim special knowledge of supernatural beings and demand they be worshiped, who become intense and unbalanced in their self-abasement before the occult mysteries of the universe—and all the rest.

Ruthlessly, Paul describes such absorption in theosophic transports as sensuous, because they are often closely allied to a spiritual indulgence and self-gratification not far removed from sensuality. He thinks the outcome is often spiritual conceit—"being puffed up without reason." There may be deliberate irony in Paul's thus subtly replacing the claim of the mystic to be inspired—inbreathed—with the crueller phrase "inflated with your own conceit!" Most of all, such people are dwelling on their own emotional experiences instead of "holding fast the Head" from whom the whole body, nourished and knit together, "grows with a growth that is from God"—not from being spuriously blown up with self-importance.

It is a poor faith that never knows its moments of ecstasy, a drab discipleship that is never stirred to wonder, love, and praise. No Christian should let the days drag into years without occasional fresh and vivid realization of the good hand of God, of thrilling answer to prayer, of the voice that guides and the strength that renews. But these private experiences, our thrills and joys, are not the rock on which we build. That rock is Christ—His word and work and person. The thrills and joys are the bonus of a life fixed on Him. We do not live for the excitements, or by them; we can live without them—but not without Him.

Strangest of all the religious shadows men have pursued is violent self-torture. The same speculative philosophy about pure Spirit and evil matter which had serious consequences for Christian thinking had dire consequences also for Christian ethics. For if all material things were inherently and incurably evil, including the body, then one could either ignore the sins of the flesh as unimportant, or—as more earnest people contended—all that belonged to the life of the flesh must be rigorously, ruthlessly, relentlessly suppressed.

This is "the rigor of devotion and self-abasement and severity to the body" (RSV) which Paul deprecates; the endless ascetic rules, "Do not handle this, do not taste that, do not so much as touch the other thing," again all of them negative rules of abstinence, avoidance, and suppression. The story of Christianity is darkened by many excesses, cruelties, and morbid revulsions from all things happy and natural and human, arising from this distorted doctrine of self-denial carried to self-torture; this unscriptural denial of the glory of creation; this un-Christian rejection of the sanctity of marriage, sex, parenthood, and childhood. The urge to be holy sometimes becomes desperate, where temptation has proved intolerable; and a passionate contempt for all things lovely and good and pure and enjoyable has seemed to some men the one escape from the world's sinful allurements.

Yet the method, like the doctrine, is false and ineffective. Only the shadow of holiness is achieved, a negative, joyless, self-protective withdrawal from family and social duty and from the need of the world. Paul declares that it does not work, it has "no value in check-ing the indulgence of the flesh" (RSV). It may even be, as the mar-ginal translation suggests, that with further irony and sharp perception, Paul says more: in so concentrating upon the sins of the flesh, ascetic self-torture does the devil's own work; in its inverted way, it is an indulgence of the flesh. At any rate, it lacks the substance of a sound and happy Christian character.

The deceptiveness of all shadows lies in their likeness to the real thing. Philosophical speculation is not unlike the deep divine wisdom which faith lays hold of; ritualism resembles real worship; mystic ex-citements are easily mistaken for the joy of God's presence; ascetic self-torture passes often for heroic self-discipline. How can we tell the shadow from the substance; how can we know the reality from the sham? Paul's tests are simple, and sufficient.

What *authority* has this practice, or that teaching, or the other pattern of worship? he asks. Does it derive from Christ, or from hu-man precepts and doctrines? Does it hold fast to the Head, the source of all direction and control for the Christian body, or does it draw you away from Him? If it is real and true, it will bind you to Him, the sole authority over loving hearts.

And what *consistency* has this practice, or that teaching, or the other pattern of worship, with what you have already experienced and professed? You died with Christ to the elemental spirits of the universe—why then listen any longer to the rules and demands that flow from that source? Be consistent with what you know, stay close to where God has already blessed you. Never, for the sake of some

glittering novelty, deny what the Lord has already done for you—
that way lies faithlessness and betrayal. Certainly there is more grace,
and truth, and joy to discover, but not in contradicting your experience, only by building upon it. "As therefore you received Christ
Jesus the Lord, so live in him . . . established in the faith, just as
you were taught . . ." (RSV). That, as you already have proved, is
substance and truth.

For one test more: what *spiritual value* has this practice, or that
teaching, or the other pattern of worship? Does it achieve anything,
or is it "empty," profitless deceit? Is it the growth that comes from
God—or merely inflated and swollen pride? Do the rules you follow
make for sound character or are they an end in themselves? For Paul,
everything in Christian life must pass this test of making men actually
more righteous, more holy, more loving, more Christlike. By its fruit
you may know it. What does not build up the saints and bear fruit to
God in godliness of life, however pretentious, is mere pretense.

Christ's authority, gospel consistency, moral value—by these we
distinguish substance from semblance, reality from self-deceit. God
keep us from pursuing shadows!

> On Christ, the solid Rock, I stand;
> All other ground is sinking sand.
> —EDWARD MOTE

The Christ-Filled Christian

16

Centered Upon Christ
COLOSSIANS 3:1-4

"The world is too much with us!" If Wordsworth felt that one hundred and sixty years ago, what would he say today? In our time, publicity invades the most private areas of life: personal tragedies are exposed to make public news; the most intimate unhappiness is probed to make popular scandal. Individual convictions and beliefs are contemptuously counted out of court by some self-appointed pollster pontificating about "majority opinion" as if that defined all truth, while individual standards of behavior and taste are ridiculed with the facile assertion that most people nowadays see no wrong in most things!

The slogans of our time well illustrate our preoccupation with public ways of thinking: expediency, the public image, the mass media, the trend of public opinion, public demand. They add up to a subtle psychological pressure that externalizes all our attitudes—our judgment, our decisions, even our conscience. We come to ply for public approval, to conform at all costs. Preachers tend to become propagandists, advertising the social benefits of Christian behavior. Church conferences become mainly concerned with how the new generation will see us, how the outsider will react to our communiques and press releases. And most of us aim, in private life, above all else to show how compatible is the Christian way of living with being a good neighbor, cultivating popularity, and blurring all distinctives that annoy.

The world is too much with us: we have given our hearts away!

Of course this preoccupation with what the world thinks is not wholly wrong. Christians have to walk circumspectly toward them that are without, and provide things honest in the sight of all men. They must become actively involved in the world of which they form a part, if they are to minister to it, and they are called to witness by life and conduct in ways that attract and explain. There can be nothing wrong in thus trying "to see oursels as ithers see us"—though the result can be extremely disconcerting.

Nevertheless, it may be well to lodge a plaintive plea, to carry a small and very square banner in a timid and peaceful demonstration, on behalf of the other side of Christian life: the hidden, inner, private side of discipleship; the peace which the world cannot give or understand; the kingdom that is not of this world; the Spirit that the world cannot receive and does not know; the wisdom that the world does not understand, else it would not have crucified the Lord of glory. It is well sometimes to remember and to defend the hidden life of the individual spirit, living by its own convictions, obedient to its own conscience, fulfilling its own life program, developing its own tastes, making its own discoveries of God and the eternal verities, without troubling too much what the world says.

It is no accident that this hidden life is emphasized in the letter to Colossae, for that church was under just such pressures to externalize its thinking and behavior. The dangerous new ideas that had captivated some minds stemmed from a novel and fascinating brand of contemporary thought being discussed in all the clubs and debated wherever men met. Some Colossian Christians were simply doing their best to be "with it," trying to adjust their faith to new ideas and restate Christianity in the current jargon, swallowing the fashionable assumptions uncritically to show how compatible they were with the gospel, intelligently understood.

And this was being done, not in a consistent endeavor to rethink their faith in order to make themselves intelligible, but with a superficial readiness to compromise, in order to make themselves indistinguishable. They were taking their cue, in all their thinking, from the world around them.

But not in thought only. One feature of this new version of Christianity was an externalizing of religious life, in conformity with the new trends. It made religion a matter of feasts and fasts, of regulation and ritual, of holy days and new moon celebrations, and all the other practices and prohibitions which the watching world, even the pagan world, would understand to be "religious" and generally approve. So the emphasis was falling upon the outward forms of godliness, rather than upon its inward power.

Paul believed that under this public pressure to conform, the Christians in Colossae were giving away more than they realized. In protest, he pleaded that they would remember that the source and the determining forces in Christian life are not external pressures but internal inspiration, not the outward circumstances but the inward

experience. We take our cue not from the world but from Christ—
the Christ within. So in chapter one he stresses the hidden secret from
which Christian life begins; in chapter two, the hidden treasure which
it enjoys; and in chapter three, the hidden control to which it bows.

The hidden secret, or "mystery," is Christ in you, the hope of
glory, the focal truth from which all Christian insight, faith, and
understanding spring. Paul would turn the attention of these Christians from slavish imitation of what all men think to the secrets which
only the men of faith share; from prevailing fashions of thought to
the "open secret" of the gospel they had learned in Christ. He would
bring their every thought into captivity to Christ, the indwelling
Teacher, the Light within the soul of all who follow the Light of the
world.

Why should we be shy of claiming this inward revelation which
only the Christian knows? Did not Jesus speak of things withheld
from the wise and prudent and revealed to babes? of the gate so con-
stricted and the way so narrow that few find it? of the kingdom that
only the reborn can enter, or even see? of the Spirit who guides the
believer into all truth, but whom the world cannot receive? If we cannot think comfortably in conformity with the world about us, it is
because we come at life a different way; we have heard another message; we have seen a star, and felt a presence, and learned that secret
of the Lord which is with them that fear Him.

The Christian is not conceited, but he is privileged and convinced.
He takes his mental cue from an indwelling Master, and all his judgments, decisions, and reactions proceed from hidden premises of
thought. He cannot but be different: the first characteristic of the
Christ-filled Christian is the mind filled with Christ.

The hidden treasure is given in Christ, in whom are hid all the
treasures of wisdom and knowledge. If that again sounds very intellectual, Paul means especially the spiritual wisdom by which the
Christian lives. His mind is full of the richness of the Christian life—
the riches of the glory of the mystery of Christ, the riches of the full
assurance of understanding, the word that dwells within us richly, and
the peace that rules our hearts most royally.

This whole letter concerns the fullness of life in Christ, the hidden
treasure of a wealthy, rewarding life laid up for us in Christ. This is
the inward enrichment of which Jesus also speaks, the pearl of great

price worth selling all to possess, the treasure hidden in the fields of
life to be discovered by those whose hearts are in the kingdom.

Nothing is more typical of Christian history than the number of
men and women who remain indifferent to—or actually seem to enjoy—the solitude and deprivation of prison life. Paul and Silas sing
at midnight in the inner cell at Philippi; Bunyan in Bedford jail dreams
of the Celestial City; Rutherfurd in exile at Aberdeen writes, "I have
the company of a Lord . . . It pleaseth Him to come and dine with
a sad prisoner . . . Christ beareth me good company"; Bonhoëffer
in a German death cell rediscovered the sources of spiritual wealth.
Not one was impoverished by being cut off from the normal channels
of nourishment: his heart was at the secret source of every precious
thing.

For the second characteristic of the Christ-filled Christian is the
heart enriched by Christ.

The hidden control is the control of Christ, seated at the right hand
of God. Our life, Paul says, is hidden with Christ in God. That is not
simply life safe from the world's hurt—Christ is not exalted for *safety!*
Nor is it life constantly renewed because lived from a great depth of
being. It is life hidden in the sense of not being easily understood by
the onlooker, mysterious, not obvious or transparent in its direction
or motives or resources, because it is directed and ruled from a hidden throne.

The Christian's aspirations are not the world's ambitions: he seeks
things above, where Christ sits at the right hand of God. The Christian's affections entwine around things above the normal valuations
of men, things above and not things on the earth. The Christian's
hopes fasten on the goals God plans, Christ's appearing to rule the
world, and our appearing with Him in glory. Inevitably, therefore,
Christian life is strange, eccentric, hidden—except to those who bow
to the same inner sovereignty and acknowledge the same inner control.

A cheap print cut from a poorly produced magazine stands framed
and prized because of its frequent rebuke. A thin, lined face has eyes
hidden, for the gaze is downcast; mouth hidden, for a hand presses
the lips in concentration. The whole look is withdrawn, the look of a
man seeking and probing deep within for the light, the wisdom, the
ideals, and the direction by which to live. It is the face of a man whose
opinions provoke controversy, but whose story has thrilled our century—Albert Schweitzer.

His brilliant career in theology and philosophy, in music and medicine, won acclaim throughout Europe, until the face of a black sculptured in Colmar city square, and an article in a missionary magazine, led to the sudden abandonment of all his academic fame, to bury himself in central Africa. Schweitzer understood that the public could not comprehend what led to such a decision, but he was dismayed at the failure of Christians to share his conviction. He found it deeply moving, even "preposterous," that people familiar with the sayings of Jesus did not better appreciate the kind of nonrational, unpopular, but absolute obedience which Jesus' command of love might call for; and he recalls with comfort that Paul "conferred not with flesh and blood" beforehand about what he would do for Christ.

This is the meaning of the withdrawn, inward-searching look: it is the expression of a man who does not seek the cue for his decisions in the reactions and pressures and valuations of the world around him but in the inward constraint of the Lord whom he loves to obey. It is a hidden control not to be explained except to those who acknowledge the same sovereignty over their lives. The third characteristic of the Christ-filled Christian is the will directed by the Christ who sits at the throne of God.

Thus mind and heart and will alike are centered upon Christ; the inner life is orientated by reference to Jesus ascended, reigning, and coming. He, at the center, is the hidden secret from which we start, the hidden treasure we enjoy, the hidden control to which we bow; and from Him as center all the circumference of our life is drawn.

In all our public concern and social awareness, our evangelistic anxiety to explain ourselves to all men, we must not forget the hiddenness of life in Christ. If we were to do so, we would lose our security, for the only answer to the outward pressure of the world is the inward constraint of life in Christ. We would lose our leadership, for the world never follows, in the end, those who do not overcome it. We would lose our testimony and have nothing fresh and authentic to say to men, descending to mere debate. We would lose our resilience, for the only cure for the drain of life is inward vitality. We would lose our hope of revival, for church renewal has ever come from within the inner life of individuals open to the moving of the Spirit.

Above all, if that inner, hidden concentration of life upon our living Lord were ever to fail among us, we would lose touch with Jesus, who strove so hard to teach us "the kingdom of God is within you."

17

Cleansed for Christ
COLOSSIANS 3:5-11

The Master said that some seed fell among thorns, and the thorns grew up and choked it. Tender seedlings, springing in the overgrown hedgerow, succumb to nature's overcrowding: the warning is clear—the fruitlessness of the preoccupied life.

A generous invitation to a great supper is churlishly refused because one had bought oxen, another had bought a field, a third had married: for each, life was overfull, to his great impoverishment. A young mother-to-be arrived at a small-town inn and found it crowded: so the King of the world was born in a stable, because His place in the world was already occupied by strangers. The spiritual peril of having "no room" is written at the threshold of the gospel. Christ will not come where He is not wanted; He cannot come where there is no place for Him.

What is true of the beginning of Christian life remains true throughout its course. Describing the Christ-filled Christian, Paul begins with the inward life centered upon Christ, and he will go on to speak of the outward life clothed with Christ, but something else has to be said, however unwelcome, if the portrait is to be faithful. The Christ-filled life cannot at the same time be filled with Christless things. To become, and to remain, filled with Christ, life must be continually cleansed of all that usurps His rightful place.

Cleansing Commenced

Christian life cannot begin until room is made for Christ: some degree of renunciation is always involved. We admire the resolute decisiveness of those first disciples who left their boats and nets and their father, and followed Jesus "immediately"; we may admire still more the courageous commitment of Matthew, who not only left his tax-collector's desk, but in a formal farewell supper to which his new-found Master was invited, took leave of his former colleagues by introducing them to Christ. On the other hand we regret those who would first await a convenient death at home, or would prolong their parting from old things, or who found the conditions of selling all and giving to the poor, too demanding.

But there may be an initial renunciation more hurtful to pride and self-esteem—the renunciation of our own fitness and worthiness to be disciples. Something in us all sympathizes with Peter's "[Lord,] Thou shalt never wash my feet" and we feel thoroughly taken down when Christ replies, "If I wash thee not, thou hast no part with me" (John 13:8). Except I wash thee: when Paul has met Christ at Damascus, and is counselled by Ananias on the first steps of the Christian way, the same demand is made: ". . . now why do you wait? Rise and be baptized, and wash away your sins, calling on his name" (Acts 22:16 RSV).

So Paul says of the Corinthian believers, recalling the ugly list of Corinthian vices—"And such were some of you. But you were washed, you were sanctified, you were justified in the name of the Lord Jesus Christ and in the Spirit of our God" (1 Corinthians 6:11 RSV). And so, without hesitation, he could affirm also of the Colossians. The gospel has borne fruit in them; they have put off the body of sin in receiving Christ's sign of God's Covenant; they were buried with Christ in baptism, and raised with Him; they no longer live as once they lived, for they have put off the old nature with its practices.

It is well to be reminded, sometimes, of that repentance and remission which together first cleansed our lives to make room for Jesus. "Without holiness no man shall see the Lord": but we have none to offer—except He first wash us, by His word, and by His blood, and by His Spirit. Only then do we begin to be clean. "If we say that we have no sin, we deceive ourselves" (1 John 1:8 RSV).

Cleansing Continued

Yet repentance and faith are no prescription for instant holiness. The initial renunciation of the world, the flesh, and the devil, not hard to make in the first flush of Christian joy, must be continually reaffirmed, often in different mood and harder circumstances. We have to leave Sodom without looking back; to escape from Egypt without lusting after her garlic and spices. Conversion must be proved by constancy, and sincerity of repentance must be shown in consistency of obedience. In baptismal terms, he who is bathed needs often to wash his feet. The believer who has died to sin in his inward attitude and resolution must "reckon dead" every separate and outward part of himself, so far as it is identified with sin. Only so can the life of Christ find room to fill his soul.

Jesus once urged that in the great crises of temptation, a man might find it profitable to his soul to—so to speak—cut off his hand, pluck out his eye, if these persistently led him into sin, so dramatically and picturesquely underlining the seriousness of sin. Paul echoes Christ's words: "Mortify all your members upon the earth"—listing the sins men commit through their bodies. Paul has already castigated severely the false conceptions that make self-torture a mark of piety, but the duty to subdue and discipline the life of the flesh that the life of the spirit might triumph, is inescapable—if life is to be filled with Christ.

Such is Paul's method of appeal for continual cleansing. Reaffirm your death with Christ; put to death all Christless things; reaffirm your resurrection with Christ, and put on all Christlike things. You have *put off* the old nature—now *put to death* all that is earthly in you—and *put away* all that lingers of the ways, habits, and attitudes that do not belong to life in Christ. In baptism you did it symbolically, even as you laid aside your soiled garments and died with Christ: maintain now and always what you then did with high intent and joy —keep doing it, all the way.

For only in the soul that is continually cleansed can Christ in His fullness continue to dwell.

The Cleansing of Chastity

When we try to define more closely the meaning of this cleansing, it is important not to miss what the apostle has in mind. In part, no doubt, he is thinking of the defilements of a pagan environment. If he looks upon these with the extra sensitiveness of a Jew toward sensual and idolatrous practices, it is also true that he is only being practical and realistic as he pictures the problems of young converts in a city like Colossae.

Paul's analysis of the prevailing permissiveness moves inwards from the outward act of immorality to the state of character it embodies—impurity; to the tone of inner life behind that character— undisciplined passion; and so to the inmost sin from which the outward act takes its rise—the evil desire, or lust. Alongside this Paul names covetousness, the pagan avarice for worldly luxury, status, and magnificence. The word means literally the insatiable lust for *more*—whatever its specific object.

In Jewish eyes, sensuality and avarice were characteristic of the gentile world, and some aspects of the teaching troubling Colossae tended to condone the pagan sins. By deliberately reminding his readers that so they once had lived, and from such ways Christ had once saved them, Paul probably hoped to reawaken the revulsion and penitence which they had felt when first the good news of Christ had kindled their hearts.

That Paul should name such perils reminds us how recent was the Colossians' conversion, how desperate the pressures among which they lived, how vulnerable all men and women are but for the grace of Christ. A Christian veneer can be very thin: if it be only a veneer, it can never protect the soul from sin. Only the constant cleansing of a deliberately renewed and reaffirmed death with Christ to evil, and resurrection with Him to newness of life, can keep the Christian unspotted from the world, "betrothed . . . to Christ . . . as a chaste bride to her one husband" (*see* 2 Corinthians 11:2), as Paul expresses it.

Few Christians in these days need to be told how vital to a Christ-filled experience is a sensitive and resolute purity. The omnipresent sensuality of modern society is a constant peril to any deepening awareness of God. If our generation is less certain of God than most generations have been, the cause is by no means wholly intellectual; "the flesh lusteth against the spirit," says Paul, and man indulges the flesh only at the cost of his spirit. Said Robert Burns:

> I waive the quantum o' the sin,
> The hazard of concealing:
> But, och! it hardens a' within,
> And petrifies the feeling!

—and he should know.

Yet chastity of mind and heart is not the only cleanness necessary to the Christ-filled soul.

The Cleansing of Charity

For not sensuality alone unfits the soul for the indwelling Christ; want of love, insensitiveness to the need and the feeling of others has the same dire effect. If Christ cannot dwell in the sensual soul, nor can He at home in the selfish heart.

That is why Paul passes at once to a second list of things to be put away—anger, wrath, malice, slander, foul talk—every one a sin against Christian fellowship. The new convert, at Colossae as everywhere else, comes through Christ into a new social context, whose law is love, whose unity is sacred, whose mutual loyalty is a necessary element in loyalty to Christ Himself. Sharply, Paul reminds the church that in her common life there can be no longer Greek and Jew, circumcised and uncircumcised, barbarian, Scythian, slave, freeman: instead, Christ is all, and He is in them all. Therefore they are one, must be seen as one, and must allow nothing to break or hinder that unity.

We know of no deep division at Colossae to call for this sharp reminder. But one feature of the teaching Paul is opposing, which was especially repugnant to his humble and outgoing soul, was its intellectual pride and exclusiveness. Another, equally evident from all references to it, was its lovelessness. That attitude of mind would as effectively preclude the fullness of Christ within the soul as any indulgence of the flesh. As Christ Himself is love, He can dwell in fullness only in the life wide open to love. Since Paul craves for every Christian at Colossae and elsewhere the fullest possible experience of the fullness of Christ, he pleads for an eager, Christlike charity of heart as urgently as he demands a sensitive, Christlike chastity of mind and soul. Both sin and selfishness are, inevitably, impoverishments of soul —bolts upon the door that shuts Christ from His due place within our hearts.

By the same token they shut us out from paradise regained. In Christlike purity and love the newness of our new nature is made plain —that "new nature which is being renewed in knowledge after the image" of Him who created it. The echo of the Eden tragedy could not be plainer, nor the promise of full restoration. The knowledge which Adam sinned to obtain, and so forfeited, and which the false philosophers at Colossae promised and could not give, that knowledge is given to the Christian in the fullness of wisdom and knowledge hidden in Christ. The divine image which Adam bore, and by his disobedience lost, this too is given again to the Christian filled with the fullness of Christ.

So the ancient curse is lifted, the verdict annulled, the loss restored. "In Him the tribes of Adam boast more blessings than their father lost." For the sake of that glorious reward, no putting away out of our lives of all things Christless can ever be too costly a preparation.

Come down, O Love divine,
Seek thou this soul of mine,
And visit it with thine own ardor glowing;
O Comforter, draw near,
Within my heart appear,
And kindle it, thy holy flame bestowing.

O let it freely burn,
Till earthly passions turn
To dust and ashes, in its heat consuming . . . .

Let holy charity
Mine outward vesture be,
And lowliness become mine inner clothing . . . .

And so the yearning strong
With which the soul will long,
Shall far outpass the power of human telling;
For none can guess its grace,
Till he become the place
Wherein the Holy Spirit makes his dwelling.

18

Clothed With Christ

COLOSSIANS 3:12-14

Matthew preserves a curious and contradictory parable which begins
with guests urgently gathered for a wedding feast, men found at the
last minute tramping the thoroughfares, "both bad and good," but
which ends with very stern punishment for one found to be without
a wedding garment. As they now stand, the closing words seem
singularly unfair, but if the final fragment be considered alone, its
point is clear: those who sup with kings should carry themselves
royally.

Clothes do not make the man, or the woman, but they do express
the character. The uniform enshrines authority; armor reveals the
soldier, the robe the priest. Clean linen often betokens the fastidious

mind, and outward charm and color suggest an inward grace and
lively imagination. The fop, the fool, and the fanciful are betrayed by
what they wear; and if want cannot help shabbiness, painstaking neat-
ness and care may serve to emphasize the thrift and pride which
refuse to make poverty an excuse. Your "habit" signifies what you are,
as well as what you wear.

Even at backsliding Sardis, not far from Colossae, there were some
later "who had not soiled their garments": it was promised that they
would walk with Christ in white, for they were worthy. In ancient
ceremony, the newly baptized walked in procession from baptistery
to Table clothed in clean garments replacing the soiled and shabby
things "put off" with the old nature and its way when they came to
Christ. Now, cleansed and reclothed, they set forth to display "the
Christian fashion," the garments of the renewed soul, the life adorned
with Christ.

Paul has been urging that those who had died with Christ should
persistently "put to death" every separate member of the old self that
was identified with sin. Now he urges that those remade by Christ
shall "put on" every separate item of the new character, piece by
piece, until they stand clothed with Christ. "For as many of you as
have been baptized into Christ have put on Christ" (Galatians 3:27
RSV). The negative goodness which puts away un-Christlike things is
not enough: it only prepares for positive good, for "putting on Christ."

Lest that become a mere poetic fancy of "looking something like
Jesus," Paul at once defines it: it means bearing in all circumstances
the character of Christ; reacting in all situations according to the
example of Christ; and fulfilling in all relationships with others, the
supreme law of Christ. That is putting on Christ.

The character of Christ is delineated in five swift strokes. *Compassion* is essentially the sympathetic spirit that is moved to feel with
others and for others, and to take their part: it is the direct opposite
of all censoriousness. *Kindness* is the outgoing generosity of mind
that longs to help, to enrich, and to make happy. *Lowliness* is not
being low, or feeling low; it is the absence of that pride which is so
easily hurt, so readily stung to retaliation. By assuming a low place
from the start, it avoids humiliation; its reactions have no aggressive-
ness, no self-assertion, no wounded dignity. *Meekness* is really the
gentle patient spirit that avoids anger and the swift, hurtful retort;
while "patience" here represents what Paul called *longsuffering,* the
ability to bear ill indefinitely, without bitterness, to "put up with" the

idiosyncrasies of others—including both their craziness and their sin!

This is not at all the kind of character which the pseudointellectuals troubling Colossae would admire, or wish to cultivate. For them, pride, cleverness, contempt for the low, the ability to defend yourself, would be more highly prized. But this is the character of Jesus: that is enough for Paul. Weak and passive though they sound, such qualities in fact display considerable maturity and consummate strength of mind.

What is more, in any group, society, or fellowship, where individuals of varying background, race, social level, education, and spiritual experience are sharing in a common life and cause, such qualities are vital. They lubricate all social intercourse; they make possible the meeting of mind with mind, heart with heart; they create the group out of the units thrown together; by means of such social cohesives the individual becomes attached, expands, and is enriched, as only one truly sharing in the life of others can ever be.

That Paul is thinking of the individual within the context of the Christian group is evident: "the elect people," "the saints," the "beloved" must in their common life manifest that Christ is in all—and that requires each for himself to put on the character of Christ the common Lord.

The example of Christ, shining the more clearly under injustice and wrong, had immediate and pressing importance in the church at Colossae. Paul will presently mention Onesimus, a slave who had stolen from his master and fled from his Colossian household, but who had now found Christ and was being sent back to put matters right. Here was an actual injury suffered by a member of the church, and one concerning which every slave master in the province would feel strongly that an example must be made. But the young man was returning as a Christian brother: much would depend on the reception he was given by the Christians at home.

Besides this, the atmosphere within the church was far from smooth. Controversy breeds irritation; hard things are said, hard to forget; imputations are implied and friendships strained. Where controversy involves deep convictions, the divisions are correspondingly painful and lasting. There is even the possibility that the pastor, Epaphras, had been criticized and his authority questioned.

Such injury and offense will surely arise, even in Christian assemblies. What can be done about them? Paul's answer is forthright: "Forbear one another, and if one has a complaint against another, forgive each other: as the Lord has forgiven you, so you also must forgive." If injury and offense seem unpreventable, in a Christian assembly they *must* be curable. Bound in a common experience of divine forgiveness, what can Christians do, but forgive as they have been forgiven?

Paul appeals not to the Lord's example only, "as the Lord has forgiven"; but to the individual's own experience of that grace exercised toward himself, "as the Lord has forgiven *you.*" We are not spectators only of Christ's pardoning love, but its undeserving recipients. The model of a forgiving spirit, and the moral compulsion to emulate it, combine in that appeal. The Christian, whose standing within the Christian society rests upon his being a redeemed, forgiven man, has really no alternative but to deal faithfully, immediately, and peaceably with every occasion of offense and division.

It is a sad comment upon human—and Christian—inconsistency that such a reaction to injury and discord cannot be taken for granted. It has to be deliberately adopted and carefully maintained, "put on" by the renewed soul, in a disciplined loyalty to the Lord's own standard of behavior.

The law of Christ, of course, is the law of love. Paul may mean that is "above all" in the sense of being most important of all, or to crown and complete all else. But Alexander Maclaren suggested love was the silken sash or belt, the final garment to be donned, holding all other garments neatly in their place. The basic thought is clear and imperative: it is Christ's own law of love which binds in one fellowship all who own Him Saviour and Lord, all for whom He is all, and in all.

It cannot be said too often that this is fundamental to *Christ's* Christianity. There is no such thing as an individual disciple; Jesus insists all the time upon the Father and His family of sons, upon the King and His circle of subjects, upon the Master and the disciple band, upon the Vine and the interconnected branches, upon the supreme rule that binds a man to the man "nigh" to him, his neighbor —a command second only to love for God. "Love one another," the Master said again in the Upper Room, thinking of the hostile world in which unyielding mutual loyalty would be their strength and witness. "Bear each one another's burdens, and so fulfil the law of Christ" (Galatians 6:2 RSV). "Owe no one anything, except to love one another . . . he who loves his neighbor has fulfilled the law" (Romans 13:8 RSV).

It was a challenging emphasis to drop into the intellectual debate at Colossae. But for Paul, obedience to the plain command of Jesus was fundamental. There could be no point arguing who Jesus was if you did not intend to do what He said; and no point either in calling Him Lord if His law was not obeyed. Without that moral submission, nothing else mattered; knowledge, conviction, doctrine, proud pretensions of "advanced Christian experience" were trivialities, or lies, if love was absent. Though a man speak with tongues human or angelic; though he had all knowledge and understood all mysteries; though he possessed the faith that removes mountains, lavished all he possessed upon the poor, was ready to be burnt for his convictions— all was *nothing,* mere sounding brass and hollow noises, without the love which Jesus requires of all who follow Him.

This "above all" is essential to "putting on Christ." Without obedience to Christ's love, a man may hug to himself the rags and tatters of Christian notions, feelings, traditions, and conventions, but he is not clothed with Christ. The supreme irony of self-deception often allows a man who cannot get on with his fellow Christians, who can never agree, or submit, or conciliate, or cooperate, or find another Christian he can unreservedly admire, to persuade himself it is because he is nearer to the Lord, more loyal to the faith, more devoted to the ways of God. Paul would retort that it can only be because he has not love —and so is nothing.

Such are the garments of the renewed soul, the character of Christ, the example of Christ, the law of Christ. The Christ-filled Christian, his inner life centered upon Christ, his mind and heart cleansed for Christ, is now clothed with Christ, and stands forth among men in radiant Christlikeness.

> I want the adorning divine
>   Thou only, my God, can bestow
> I want in those beautiful garments to shine
>   Which distinguish Thy household below.

Here, truly, is a wedding garment fit for the presence of the King. Not Solomon, in all his glory, was arrayed like one of these!

The Christ-Filled Life

19

Overflowing Within the Church
COLOSSIANS 3:15-17

The surest sign that you are carrying a full bucket is—wet feet. A vessel is only really full when it begins to overflow: so the proof of a Christ-filled life, the value of a Christ-filled life, and ultimately the purpose of a Christ-filled life, lie in the outflow into other lives of the riches we ourselves enjoy.

That is why John adds to one tremendous declaration of Jesus— "As the living Father hath sent me, and I live by the Father: so he that eateth me, even he shall live by me" (John 6:57)—a second equally wonderful promise: "If any one thirst, let him come to me and drink. He who believes in me, as the scripture has said, 'Out of his heart shall flow rivers of living water'" (John 7:37, 38 RSV). The outflow proves the inflow, and demonstrates the fullness.

That, too, is why Paul passes, in this letter to Colossae, from expounding the fullness of Christ to the fullness of the Christ-filled Christian, and then immediately to the Christ-filled life and its amazing overflow in all the situations in which the Christian is set. At church, at home, at work, and in private worship, on the street, among our friends, in Christian work, the fullness of life and joy, of grace and power, of wisdom and of love, which we have received, should *pour out,* in godliness, in graciousness, in gratitude, and in genuine goodness.

No gift or blessing of the Christian life is ever meant for my heart alone. Of what profit is it, to myself or to the world around me or to God, that my soul should be centered on Christ, cleansed for Christ, clothed with Christ, filled by Christ, unless in consequence my life contributes positively and energetically to all that He would do for men? As ever, the hymnist keeps the emphasis right:

O fill me with Thy fullness, Lord,
    Until my very heart o'erflow
In kindling thought and glowing word,
    Thy love to tell, Thy praise to show.
                    —FRANCES RIDLEY HAVERGAL

The fullness of Christ is not given us to enjoy, but to enjoy the use of.

And where should we expect to see the Christ-filled life first over-flow, but in our Christian circles, our assemblies, fellowships, churches, groups; at Christian worship, in conference, through all specifically religious activities? That is where Paul begins his description of the overflowing life.

Everything in the passage points to this. Paul has just been de-scribing the qualities that make for smooth cooperation among Chris-tians, and for reconciliation of divisions; these qualities are clearly set in contrast to the vices that divide and alienate—anger, wrath, malice, lies, and the rest. The whole paragraph is addressed to the people of God—elect, holy, beloved—all terms applied in the Old Testament to the chosen Israel. The focal verse declares this social theme uncompromisingly: "In Christ there cannot be Greek and Jew, circumcised and uncircumcised, barbarian, Scythian, slave, free man, but Christ is all, and in all."

As if this were not enough, Paul stresses that the Colossians were "called in the one body"; they must teach and admonish one another in mutual edification, and sing together in God's praise—plainly referring to the corporate worship of the congregation. Paul would have each individual Colossian Christian so filled with Christ that the common worship, fellowship, and activity of the assembly is overflowing with the grace and power and joy of the Lord. Indeed, it is very doubtful whether Paul would distinguish as sharply as we tend to do, the Christian's individual life from his corporate life. What *is* a Christ-filled church, but a church of Christ-filled Christians?

Yet sometimes the quality of the church's common life falls sadly below that of its finest members. Hence the three perceptive exhorta-tions:

Let the peace of Christ rule in your hearts.

Of course it is within the heart of each member of the group that the legacy of Christ is to be received: but Paul's plea is that the peace indwelling the heart of each Christian shall be allowed to dominate, to discipline, to control, the life of the community. He expressly adds, "to which indeed you were called in the one body" (RSV), to emphasize that his concern at the moment is for that common peace.

The peace of Christ should settle all conflicts. To preserve that peace must be a clear obligation upon each member, and when difficult choices have to be made, that peace should "sit as umpire" on divisive questions. So some translations preserve Paul's metaphor, drawn from the Greek athletic games. That decision should be reached, that choice made, which shall best promote and preserve the peace Christ gives. *What destroys Christ's peace is bound to be wrong.* Everything that divides, if necessary everyone who divides, must be excluded for the sake of the peace of Christ.

Paul's direction is clear but it is not easy. Christians are both conscientious and contentious, and neither makes for easy compromise. So Paul adds, "Be agreeable, pleasant, good-natured, easy to get on with." So, most probably, we should understand his word, rather than "Be thankful." He is perhaps echoing a Hebrew phrase in Proverbs, and anticipating something he will write later. At any rate, no one who has sought to work alongside awkward, aggressive, disagreeable Christians will question the need of such an exhortation, if the peace of Christ is to rule the Christian assembly. More divisions arise from lack of graciousness than from lack of faithfulness to truth.

At first sight, it may seem pedestrian to look first, for evidence of the fullness of Christ overflowing a Christian group, to an everyday, domestic matter like keeping the peace together. But one thing is certain: where that peace is absent, *nothing at all* of the fullness of Christ will be manifest in any other way.

Let the word of Christ dwell in you richly.

Social fellowship and personal friendship are not the only, or even the main, expressions of Christian solidarity. A teaching and witnessing ministry is a necessary function of any Christian group—the exploration, exposition, and expression of the saving word in preaching, study, and testimony. So the group is nourished, guided, and enriched by the gospel that its members share.

So Paul turns to consider the freedom afforded to the word of Christ to do its work within the Colossian congregation. Because of the atmosphere of controversy, this teaching and admonishing was the more important; but for the same reason it must be done "in all wisdom" as well as faithfully, that the truth well spoken may convince, correct, instruct, subdue. We are reminded of the freedom and spontaneity of early Christian worship, as prophets, elders, teachers, pastors, evangelists took their parts in the service, each speaking by the Spirit a divine message. Paul would have them earnest and responsive to what the Lord will say: "let the word of Christ dwell richly among you."

But not in speaking only; in praise too, as with glad and thankful hearts they unite in "sacred song, festal praise, and solemn ode," making melody in their hearts to God. Here, too, let it be the word of Christ that prompts your singing. The variety named suggests a rich repertoire of worship-praise shared by the congregation—the distinctions would be pointless if Paul were thinking only of "the silent singing of the happy Christian heart." The apostolic church, it has been said, was emphatically a singing church; and every great revival and reformation has evoked its burst of song. Perhaps here too Paul asks for "pleasant agreeableness" in sweet singing, but his chief concern is that Christian worship, whether in speech or in song, shall be enriched by the word of Christ.

Paul speaks so often of "the unsearchable riches of Christ," the riches of assured understanding, the riches of the glory of the mystery, the treasures of wisdom and knowledge, and now of the word dwelling in us richly, that one suspects some subtle contrast, either with the material loss he sustained by becoming a Christian, or with the poverty of spiritual experience in Judaism. More probably, he is thinking of the foolish and conceited claims to an advanced and superior philosophy put forward by the innovators at Colossae. It may well be that the spiritual hunger and dissatisfaction which gave deviationist notions and speculative heresies their opportunity were the consequence of a poor grasp of the gospel, despite all their pastor's efforts, and a too emotional, too superficial worship.

Paul would have their minds, and their services, enriched with the truth because it does not occur to well-nourished, well-taught Christians to seek spiritual excitements and intellectual fancies somewhere else. When the fullness of Christ is overflowing in the worship services of the church, hearts, minds, and spirits are abundantly satisfied.

Do everything in the name of the Lord Jesus.

Happy fellowship and enriching worship do not quite exhaust the functions of the Christian community: inevitably, it *acts* both individ-

ually and corporately as representative of Christ. Even the private
actions of the Christian are read by the onlooker as examples of the
church's policy, but Paul is thinking of the united actions of the
Christian group within a town or village. He would have every deed
and word worthy of the Name which the church bears and represents.

In a score of ways, the Christian group reacts toward the surround-
ing, watching world: in witness, protest, and example; in service
prompted by compassion, good neighborliness, love; sometimes in
resistance to the point of persecution; at other times cooperating with
all good men to serve the social ideal. As each Christian is salt, light,
and leaven in his pagan environment, so the Christian community,
also, is a cell, a pressure group, an activist society for the Kingdom of
God, a refuge for the friendless and the lost, a city set on a hill.

One overriding principle, Paul suggests, must absolutely govern all
their decisions and reactions, their work and their relationships: they
must be deeds, decisions, and reactions to which in all sincerity they
can subjoin the Name that is above every name, the Name they first
confessed in baptism, that worthy Name by which they were called.
If that sanctifying Name controls all their behavior toward the world,
the fullness that the Name represents will fill their united life and work
with the fragrance and power of the Lord they love.

Detailed directions for Christian living in every age are impossible
to frame: Paul offers a principle of almost universal range, clarity, and
validity: *whatever* you do, do all in the name of the Lord, Jesus.
What honors His name must be right, and what is right in His sight
will be blessed with the fullness of His truth and grace and glory.

Such is a Christ-filled church—an assembly, situated in any village,
town, suburb or city, of Christ-filled men and women, adorned with
Christ's character, modeled on His example, willingly subject to His
law; a society which in its common life is ruled by His peace, indwelt
and enriched by His word, and worthy to bear His name. In such a
church, the fullness of Christ first overflows—though the streams will
run beyond its life. There hearts will be nourished, lives refilled,
wounds healed, the tempted armed, the sad uplifted, the lame walk,
the blind see, the dumb sing, the lonely find friends; and the Lord
will add to such a church constantly those who are being saved.

It sounds an impossible ideal, yet there is nothing wrong with the
modern church which revival will not put right. Only revival must
come from within, not from without—from the overflow in fellowship

of the fullness experienced by Christ-filled Christians. There is no
other way.

20

Overflowing in the Christian Home
COLOSSIANS 3:18-21

Home may be "the nursery of the infinite" and "heaven for beginners,"
but for all that it seems a long step down from the cosmic fullness of
Christ to talk of domestic Christianity. The opening of this epistle to
Colossae is so extremely lofty, far-ranging and glorious in its affirmations of faith, that discussion now of "religion in the kitchen" is almost
bound to be an anticlimax!

Yet that descent to everyday duty is entirely characteristic, not only
of Paul but of Christianity. Jesus will never allow the retreat on the
Mount of Transfiguration to last for long; we come down relentlessly
to the valley with its epileptic children and its cries for help. "Faith
which works by love" is Paul's definition of the Christian religion, and
without the working and the love, faith would have no reality. To him,
it is no change of theme to pass from the fullness of Christ and the
Christ-filled life to speak of family life. For the Christ-filled life must
show its quality in near and earthly matters, or not at all. It is not
needed in heaven.

But for some people, a much more serious descent in the level of
discussion will appear in the way in which Paul writes of domestic
relationships. On the unity and equality in Christ of people of all races,
levels of education, and social status, he has spoken with the liberal
and generous tone congenial to modern minds. But when he speaks of
husband and wife, parent and child, he drops suddenly to the language
of subjection, of obedience, of rank preserving privilege—male over
female, old over young. That is a serious criticism, and deserves serious consideration.

The virtues of subjection, obedience, and discipline held far larger
place in Christianity in former ages than they do today, when we are
almost afraid to mention them. Both in Judaism and in apostolic

Christianity, the essence of sin was held to lie in the self-assertion of the human will against the will of God. Man had misused his freedom, directing it against his Maker: that was his fall, his predicament, and his final condemnation. Salvation, therefore, must involve submission; only under God's rule could man find unity, security, and hope.

In Judaism, this was firmly expressed in Law. In the teaching of the Master, it is transmuted into the theme of the kingship of the heavenly Father, and submission to a loving reign. In the apostolic teaching, the same insight underlies the proclamation that Jesus is Lord, and the call to the obedience of faith. Plainly, this element of the gospel can never be ignored: where disobedience has destroyed, only obedience can save; where self-will, foolishly asserted against the Source of all our welfare, has brought us to ruin, only surrender can restore security, only subjection to God's will can keep us safe.

But while this may be the rationale of Christian obedience, it is very clear that subjection toward God in Christ is one thing: obedience and subjection within the Christian home is quite another. We must look further.

What precisely does Paul say about husband and wife?

Women probably had in general a lower status in society in the ancient East than they enjoy in the modern West—though the contrast is sometimes exaggerated. In the vulnerable years of childbearing, the woman is the more dependent for protection and provision and possesses inevitably less freedom of independent action. But Paul here is neither reproducing Jewish tradition nor appealing to natural circumstance. He lifts the relationship of husband and wife to a new level, in three distinct ways.

(1) No such thing as "absolute submission" is in Paul's mind: subjection is expressly limited to what is fitting in the Lord. The conscience clause is still more strongly expressed in similar counsel in Ephesians, where the wife's "subjection" is paralleled to obedience to Christ—it is of that *kind*. Paul avoids the word *obey:* he is thinking of the acceptance of clearly defined rank and function within an ordered family. He speaks in the same terms of the relation of men, women, Christ and God, in writing to Corinth, and in the same terms again when writing of the Christian citizen in the state. Only what may fairly be asked, under Christ, as necessary to the good order of the home, is implied. In such an order, the right of decision, in any matter, belongs to the partner who carries main responsibility for that matter.

In matters affecting the home as a whole, the right of decision rests with the one who carries ultimate responsibility for the home as a whole.

It seems likely that, at Colossae as at Corinth, the new freedom and dignity of women within the church had led to scandal in the eyes of outsiders; Paul's advice then would be similar to that he gives about behavior at church and in dress: give no ground for offense. But basically, Paul asks simply for the acceptance of order, difference of function, and responsible decision.

(2) Even more significant than this limiting of submission to things conscientiously defensible is the requirement of a reciprocal obligation by the husband: "husbands, love your wives" was sheer novelty, when presented as a religious *demand*. Even in Judaism a woman could not divorce her husband, for disloyalty or anything else; a husband could demand that his wife love him only, but she could not demand his love. A new notion of domestic equality gleams in this emphasis upon reciprocal obligation. Whatever self-abnegation is involved in acceptance of rank within the family is shorn of all indignity when set within such love. In Ephesians, Paul requires husbands to love their wives as Christ loves the church and gave Himself for it—and on that premise counsels the wife's subjection. If Christlike love be withheld, subjection cannot be demanded in Christ's name: the home has ceased to be a Christian home.

(3) Paul's third comment on the marital relationship is specific to the point of bluntness. Woman's physical and economic weakness, compared with man, had created a sexual tradition which gave to the husband both power and right over the wife's person, to which she was expected meekly to submit. Paul simply forbids the harsh, overbearing demand. Peter, likewise, requires that Christian husbands "dwell with their wives with understanding and reasonableness." Christianity was steadily imposing a new standard of sexual behavior within marriage as well as outside it. By that forthright insistence upon conscience, reciprocal love, and sexual consideration, it was creating the climate in which its new principle could flourish—in Christ Jesus "there is neither male nor female" (Galatians 3:28)—both are one in Him.

All in all, there is no possible doubt that in Paul's counsel woman has gained far more than she seems to lose, and the order of a Christian home is set firmly under the rule of Christ. In such a home, His fullness can overflow in joy.

What precisely does Paul say about parent and child?

Judaism had well understood that character training and social morality begin within the home, and Paul realized that the best school for Christians is the Christian family. And here again, between young and old, the obligation is mutual.

(1) The child's obedience is that of discipline rather than of accepted rank and function. The child begins its moral education by obeying instructions and following example long before it can understand the reasons for the rules. Such understanding, leading to assent, is always the goal; the rules should be reasonable and explained as persuasively as possible; but even so, until insight comes, obedience must guide and guard the growing life.

Those who object to this do not always realize what a relief it is to a child to have others' firmness to lean upon and to shelter within. Too often, weak parents shirk responsibility by pretending to "let the children choose" in freedom of self-determination, merely transferring their responsibility for decision and consequences on to the immature mind and conscience. Direction and obedience are far kinder and safer guides, until maturity is ready to take over.

The child within the Christian circle is reminded that such honor toward parents is "pleasing in the Lord"—an appeal to the child's own growing response to the gospel and its own love for Jesus. Paul reminds the children at Ephesus that such obedience is "right." Perhaps he is hinting that even if parents are unreasonable, overbearing, perhaps unconverted, the Christian's obligation to *be* a Christian in one's home remains unchanged.

(2) But this is no charter of unlimited parental authority. The obedience to others' judgment which is pleasant in the young child is pitiable, and perilous, in the adolescent. The parent's first duty is so to exercise authority as to prepare for self-reliant responsibility. The worst of all parental failures is to demand implicit obedience, refusing explanations, denying all discussion of moral rules as the child grows older, withholding freedom and responsibility far too long by clinging to authority in the name of "love" or "gratitude" long after the child has challenged and rejected it—and then to blame the adolescent for being stupid, rebellious, and irresponsible. What else could such a child be?

(3) Of course the problem is how and when and in what realms to pass responsibility for decision gradually to the growing child. The

only possible answer is, as soon as he is ready to discuss and understand the principles involved. Paul mentions expressly the two chief
dangers. One, that the strong-willed, adventurous, daring child may
be provoked to rebellion by harsh authoritarianism; this is the "exasperation" evoked by overstrictness and a continual clash of wills. The
other danger, equally serious, is that the sensitive, introspective, timid
child may be crushed by discouragement and repeated rebuke into
perpetual fear and distrust. In the one case, parents will be responsible
for the undisciplined, antisocial, defiant young adults they turn loose
upon society; in the other, parents will be equally responsible for the
weak character, vulnerable to every pressure of the world and prey
to every exploiter of evil, which their treatment produced.

Remembering that so far as we know Paul had no children, his insight and shrewdness are remarkable. But he grew up in a strict Jewish
home, surrounded by all the allurements which a pagan city, with its
temples, soldiery, athletic games and theaters, would offer to a lively
imagination and a curious mind. Perhaps he knew from experience
both the rebellious exasperation with family rules, and the feeling of
being vulnerable, unarmed, inexperienced, as he grew away from
that sheltering discipline, among students at Jerusalem.

The ideal Paul presents so briefly is hard to excel. The husband
loyal and gentle, while accepting ultimate responsibility; the wife
loved, accepting lesser responsibility within an equal partnership;
children learning their moral lessons by obedience before they have
to understand and decide for themselves; parents exercising authority
always with an eye to coming freedom, strength, and maturity in
their children; and all within a clear and shared loyalty to the Lord
they love—is there any better basis for family life, or for society?

But Paul's purpose reaches beyond family counseling. He is thinking still of the fullness of Christ, flowing out in lives filled with Christ,
overflowing not only in church but at home, embracing the family
within the grace and love and power of the gospel. Through such
Christian homes, scattered throughout the Empire, the meaning of the
Christian message would be made visible in a new standard of domestic unity and a new depth of personal happiness. Many would be
envious, and by inquiry be led to faith.

Just as surely, through such Christian families the fullness of Christ
flowed forward into a new generation, as children grew in the nurture
and instruction of the Lord. Though Paul may have had no long view

of Christian history, his Jewish training made him see the future in the children. There was nothing automatic in the process, as Judaism tended to think; but as parent and child are faithful to Christian standards, the faith would be kindled, and the fullness of Christian life flow on, through the immeasurably powerful influence of a Christian home.

21

Overflowing Through the Working Day
COLOSSIANS 3:22-4:1

In the days when the astonishing success of Christianity in the world demanded some explanation, even for pagans, a Christian writer offered, along with the persuasion of prophecies fulfilled and the intrinsic reasonableness of the gospel, this illuminating comment: "Our Lord urged us by patience and meekness to lead all from shame and the lusts of evil, and this we have to show in the case of many who have come in contact with us, who were overcome and changed from violent and tyrannical characters, either from having watched the constancy of their Christian neighbors, or from having observed the wonderful patience of Christian travelers when overcharged, or from doing business with Christians." That is Justin the Martyr, in the second century.

"Doing business with Christians"—an evangelistic agency! Professor John Foster's comment is just: he remarks that we do not know who founded the churches in some of the greatest cities of the ancient world; often they were not apostles, nor full-time missionaries, but ordinary Christians "who carried their religion with them as they went about their business."

There could be no finer testimony to the persuasive power of a life filled with Christ, overflowing in witness, uprightness, kindness, and radiance, through the ordinary tasks and personal contacts of every working day. But Justin was thinking, obviously, of Christian business men, travelers, agents, and professional people: Paul is thinking of slaves and their masters. Christian witness through work may be convenient and influential for those in the greater freedom of managerial and professional occupations and in self-chosen vocations; for those in menial, repetitive, and repressive work, the opportunities are far fewer. To be a Christian while being a slave is surely quite impossible! Paul insists that it is not.

Christianity took centuries too long to get rid of slavery. But it did not take long to change it. Despite the dangers of inciting slaves to an assertion of freedom which in many households could mean instant death; despite, too, the danger of identifying Christianity with revolutionary slave-emancipation movements, which could have frightened Roman society into exterminating the church, much was accomplished. The assertion that in Christ "there cannot be . . . slave, free man, but Christ is all, and in all" (RSV) was itself revolutionary, and implied the exclusion of slavery from any future Christian society.

To require of the Christian slave an honest and diligent day's work for conscience' sake, and of the Christian master that he acknowledge the slave's right to Christian treatment, was to transform the master-slave relationship entirely. To teach the slave that in the Lord's sight he is a free man, with the free man's expectation of reward for work well done, and to teach the master that in the Lord's sight he is a slave, with a Master in heaven, was to attack the whole institution at its inmost center—the slave's inner sense of humiliation and personal degradation and the master's equally corrupting sense of tyrannical power, possession, and superiority. The Master in heaven is the judge, and the example, of all masters among men.

This is not Christian charity alleviating a sorry situation. It is the forthright insistence that in Christ there can be no slave or free man. As Maclaren excellently says, "Charity likes to come in and supply wants which would never have been felt had there been equity." Paul, one feels sure, would have cried "Hear, hear!"

It may be that the defection of the slave, Onesimus, from the Christian master, Philemon, in the Colossian district, had raised the whole issue of slavery in a Christian household, but the principles involved apply in some degree to every Christian's daily employment. If Christianity can transfigure slavery, it can transfigure anything—no task is so lowly, or so dispiriting, that Christ cannot make it more tolerable, and a Christian attitude make it a vocation. We may note then, for ourselves in very different circumstances, what Paul has to say.

For the man who earns his livelihood
by working under others' direction:

To the employed man, Paul urges that daily work be wholehearted, honest, dedicated to Christ. "Singleness of heart," Paul explains, means "without duplicity"; it implies not working only when the master's eye is upon you, or merely to gain advantage over others by unfairly wooing favor, or by doing well only those parts of the work which can be inspected. As Paul's word is translated elsewhere, it suggests doing your day's work "generously."

We know that some slaves were taking advantage of more lenient Christian masters. Both the First Epistle of Peter and the First Epistle to Timothy call for "all respect": "those who have believing masters must not be disrespectful on the ground that they are brethren." This attitude is wrong, and Paul warns that He who rewards faithfulness will also punish wrongdoing, in the slave and menial no less than in the master. The weak self-pity which pleads for mercy on the ground that the slave is poor and ignorant, not morally responsible, Paul brushes aside. It was not only untrue, but perilous. It denied the principle of the slave's spiritual dignity, his equal responsibility in Christ, upon which rested the promise of future freedom and social equality. Similarly, Peter has no sentiment to waste on the dishonest slave: "For what credit is it, if when you do wrong and are beaten for it you take it patiently?" (1 Peter 2:20 RSV).

The dedication of all daily work to Christ implies not only that the character of the earthly master is irrelevant to the Christian worker's duty, but that all such daily work can be made a vocation. "You serve the Lord Christ" when you work well. Said a young Christian girl, monotonously tending a milk-bottling machine, when asked about her faith and her work: "I think each morning of the hundreds of babies who will be fed that day, and I pray that nothing I do, or let pass, will harm any one of them." To the Christian slaves at Corinth, Paul writes, ". . . let every man, wherein he is called, therein abide with God" (1 Corinthians 7:24). With such motives, and such company, the most menial task may be blessed.

So Jesus, too, counseled the transfiguration of whatever a man is compelled to do, by the willing acceptance of the compulsion; that leaves the doer free, dignified, and good-humored. He was speaking of the compulsory service of the occupying soldiery, required of every male Jew. Go the second mile of your own accord, and you have pre-

served, and asserted, your freedom of action! The same attitude of
acceptance and dedication can transform every compulsion into vocation. Even for a slave, the cringing, resentful mood is resolved, and
the day's work is done for Christ, a living testimony to His presence
and His grace—and all life is different.

What then has Paul to say?

For the man who earns his livelihood
by organizing the work of others:

We must remember that Paul's letter is intended to be read publicly
at a meeting of the church: the assurance given to the slave of the
dignity and value of his labor is made openly in the presence of masters and others. There is implied, therefore, the clear and public recognition of equal spiritual dignity, and mutual responsibility, between
employer and employed. That was no platitude in the first century!
Paul spells out its meaning in two explicit demands.

The master is to afford his servant *justice,* that which on any general and impartial view will be seen to be right. And since general
rules rarely apply equally to every individual, he must also afford to
each servant *fairness,* that which is fitting in individual circumstances
and right in a particular case. Both requirements would be, in the
eyes of most slave masters, quite preposterous. But Paul insists upon
both equity and consideration. Any punishment must be just; any
accusation proved; any special circumstances weighed; the rights of
the servant, as man and as Christian, fully preserved. The different
functions of employer and employee in the economic machine do not
at all affect the intrinsic value and inalienable sacredness of human
personality.

Paul's final, brief phrase is equally weighted with meaning: "knowing that you also have a Master in heaven" (RSV). That sudden,
solemn reminder must press the conscience of every Christian with
power over other lives. The example of Jesus, Master of us all, as to
what being master implies, is set plainly before the employer; while
the warning that the employer's treatment of others is subject to his
Master's scrutiny and judgment, is clearly implied. Perhaps actual
words of Jesus are in Paul's mind: ". . . with what judgment ye
judge, ye shall be judged" (Matthew 7:2). Those who exercise power
with harshness, severity, or any want of sympathy, can in fairness
expect no different treatment from the Master in heaven: as a man
hopes for mercy, he must learn to be merciful.

We must remember that the wider application of Christian principles to modern economic problems of production, distribution, consumption—to investment, employment, and organization for united action—is a vast subject for which the counsel sent to Colossae can offer no guidance. Paul is concerned with the individual Christian's faithfulness in his daily work, and with the personal relationship of master and worker within the Christian community and before a watching pagan society. It may well be that many wider issues turn at last on these two—the attitude of the worker to his work, and the personal equation between employer and employed; but it is of these, simply, that Paul writes.

And his deepest intention arises from the letter as a whole. Paul longs that the fullness of Christ, flowing into the Christian heart of master and slave alike, shall overflow, beyond Christian church and Christian home, into Christian daily labor and so outwards to society. In this way, the fullness offered in Christ will begin to change the social atmosphere, transform social tradition and prejudices, as more and more Christians show Christ's standards and spirit in the way they do their daily work. Only so will those who never attend a Christian church or visit a Christian home be confronted with the grace and truth of Christ as they "do business with Christ-filled Christians."

As we began with Justin the Martyr in the second century, we may well close with another great leader, Clement of the third century. Clement worked in one of the greatest seaports of the ancient world, Alexandria. His congregation and his friends were mainly concerned in the commerce and transport of that bustling center of world trade.

Like most people, Clement knew the great merchant houses by their trade signs as much as by their names, and he disliked the symbols which some of them had chosen—pictures of heathen gods— Venus, Bacchus, Mars; a sword, or a dagger or spear; wine cups, and other reminders of feasting and luxury. Christians, Clement said, are not idolators; they do not indulge in armed violence; they are not drunkards and gluttons. Why should not their signs and signet rings express what they truly are? "Let our seals be a dove, or a fish, or a ship scudding before the wind, or a ship's anchor." The dove signified the Spirit; the word *fish* spells out the Christian confession, "Jesus Christ, Son of God and Saviour"; the ship is the ark of salvation, whose yardarm and foremast make a cross; the anchor is our hope in Christ.

When our daily work proclaims who and what we are; when we let

Christ preach from our boat as He did from Peter's; when once again people are "overcome and changed" simply by "doing business with Christians"—then once more the progress of Christianity in the world will astonish and bewilder those who watch. The fullness of Christ will be finding outlet in everything we do or say or make or buy or sell or teach or offer in service. Christ shall possess our working day, and every day shall be another Lord's day.

22

Overflowing at Private Prayer
COLOSSIANS 4:2-4

It is a searching question whether perhaps many of us do not have *too many* opportunities for Christian fellowship, worship, and instruction. Too many, that is, for our spiritual health. Would our understanding of God be wiser, our inmost grasp of God be firmer, our peace with God be deeper, if we were compelled to rely entirely, not on the public means of grace but on the private springs of prayer?

To be a Christian in a pagan world was a lonely experience. The Christian slave in a great heathen household, the Christian soldier in a Roman barrack room, the only believer in a ship's idolatrous crew, the one Christian convert in a Jewish family—each would have a hard time. And not only because of outward scorn and threats: even more because of inward isolation and want of resources. There was no New Testament to pore over and delight in—even if one could read. Meetings of Christians were rare; even the weekly memorial feast was not always available to the less fortunate and free. Trustworthy friends were often few.

At the beginning, there was no building set apart for retreat, and no day when all were free to assemble with the saints. That Christian life survived amid such spiritual drought and under such pressures is itself a miracle of apostolic care of souls.

Christian life is safest when the outward pressures of society, of temptation, of fear and loneliness, of contention and scorn, are balanced by inward pressures generated by the soul's private life with God. Against the full heart, the world has no weapon; when joy and faith and courage run high, when the sense of God's blessing is fresh upon the soul and gratitude fills the mind, temptations are helpless. It needs a positive enthusiasm for God and all things good, welling up from within, to hold life invulnerable. When the storm beats high, and the war with evil presses hard:

> I want a godly fear,
> A quick discerning eye
> That looks to Thee when sin is near,
> And sees the tempter fly:
> A spirit still prepared,
> And armed with jealous care,
> For ever standing on its guard
> And watching unto prayer.
> —CHARLES WESLEY

That expresses precisely what Paul says to the Colossians about their individual strife against the evil of the world. All that he has written in this letter about the fullness that dwells in Christ; all that he has said about the fullness of the Christian life that remains rooted in the fullness of Christ, comes down at last to this: the life is filled, and overflows, only when the heart is constantly open to the things that are above. Only then are the inward resources of a richly renewed faith and love, strength and joy, more than enough to withstand the outward pressures of an evil time.

This is the real meaning of that counsel, so frequent in the New Testament, to be *constant* in prayer. "Men ought always to pray" the Master said; and He told two stories, one about a judge reluctant to hear a case, the other about a neighbor reluctant to help a friend, to illustrate how, despite difficulties, persistence may gain its end. A man may need sometimes to seek, as well as to ask, and even on occasion to knock as well, if he would receive, and find, and enter in. For persistence in prayer is frequently the proof of earnestness; and often it prunes impulsive desires to better understanding and deeper patience.

So Paul urges Christians to pray at all seasons, and constantly, and again, unremittingly. Everyone prays when the need is urgent or the mood is right: really Christian prayer is the constant discipline of a heart open Godwards—whatever the circumstance, whatever the mood, because a grateful and dependent spirit has built a steadfast habit of prayerfulness into character. This is the point at which the soul's fullness is restored. Out in the busy world the heart may still lay hold of Christ, but in the quiet moment of inward retreat and devotion, His fullness flows again into our emptiness—and overflows.

If men would always pray, they need not faint. Even Jesus found that angels ministered to Him, in the garden beneath the trees at the place of prayer.

That reference to the garden illumines another word of Paul: about being "watchful in prayer." It was in Gethsemane that the Master coupled these two imperatives, *watch* and *pray*. Alertness, vigilance, was a key theme of the earliest counseling of Christian converts, as necessity required it should be. If renewal of strength is the first spiritual value of constant prayer, the sharpening and sensitizing of conscience is certainly the second. "Blessed are those servants whom the Master finds awake . . ."(Luke 12:37 RSV)—and foolish those who in a world like ours, beset with subtle evils and unremitting temptation, allow mind and conscience to slumber in prayerlessness.

The unwelcome truth is that our lack of prayer is more often due to uneasiness of conscience than to independence of attitude. We know that if we pause to pray, some things will accuse us, some things demand to be put right, some clamor to be confessed. Yet the fullness of the blessing of Christ cannot flow in and through us unless the channels be kept clear. Pray constantly, vigilantly, says Paul, that in the face of every allurement, conflict, and demand, you may be "complete in Him."

Brief though this counsel is concerning private devotion, Paul notices two ways in which even private prayer can be narrow, inward-looking, and something less than Christian. If we concentrate only on what we want, making of prayer a mere recital of requests, then our quiet time with God can become arid and unrewarding. We do not escape our need, but remain, even while we are praying, prisoners of our discontent.

Deliberately, therefore, Paul adds "with thanksgiving." Never ask for something more without giving thanks for what you have! That way, the present need is set within the pattern of God's astonishing provision, through the days and years, in measureless ways. So the immediate want seems less urgent; that it will be met becomes so obvious that we rise from prayer with confidence, thanking God now for good yet to be received.

Since Paul's theme is the fullness of life in Christ, thanksgiving ought to figure largely in his thought: but none of his repeated references to it is more perceptive than this. Private prayer can become so plaintive, self-pitying, full of the sense of inadequacy. Sometimes we are tempted to measure its sincerity by the intensity of negative feeling, the sense of poverty, which it generates! Paul will have none of this. Pray your needs into possessions, by all means, but private moments of devotion are occasions for praise and adoration, for telling God our love, for noticing His goodness and continuing mercies, for listening, too, and sometimes for silently rejoicing that He is our God.

Then the need we knelt to ask gets lost in worship, and fulfilled in joy. Sometimes we forget to ask it—and God grants it just the same!

The second way in which private devotion can be narrow and inward-looking is by becoming self-centered. "Pray for us," Paul says, again perceptively. Lonely, beset, tempted you may be—but so are others: remember them. Prayer is always selfish where there is no intercession, and perhaps selfishness in prayer is the deepest selfishness of all.

The situation is illuminating. In their sheltered, remote valley, the Colossian Christians were facing their local difficulties and fighting their limited battles for Christ. Away at the other end of the province, or even of the Empire, Paul the ambassador for Christ stands, in peril, on the very front line of the same incessant warfare. Around Paul, and alongside him in other places, are other valiant contenders for the faith. The Colossian converts must not forget their fellow soldiers and fellow sufferers. To pray only for themselves would be inexcusable when the whole church is under pressure.

Thus, in Paul's vision, each ordinary, lonely Christian on his knees is linked to the leaders on the frontiers of the kingdom; each private prayer time is part of the battle for the truth. A little, old, silent lady trudged to church each Sunday from her little cottage at the far end of a small Welsh village, returning to a lonely room to spend most of the week unseen and unregarded. A limited life, and insignificant! Yet on her death the drawers of her kitchen table were found crammed with letters from all corners of the world, with names, facts, stories, requests for prayer, from missionaries of many labels and loyalties, linking this quiet, pious soul to Christians and non-Christians, nurses, patients, doctors, teachers, scholars, in many lands. Her private prayers embraced the world.

> And so the whole round earth is every way
> Bound by chains of gold about the feet of God—

and private devotions become as wide as the eternal love.

Paul has not forgotten his central theme. The fullness of Christ still fills his mind—and how imaginatively! The isolated, lonely Christian, shut in with his Lord, in moments snatched from the busy day, or from the all-too-short hours of a slave's allotted rest, offers his eager prayer. That praying heart, that devoted moment, becomes at once another outlet, *another point of overflow,* where all the resources of wisdom, love, and power that are in Christ may pour forth, into his own heart, into his fellow servants, into some personal friend, into another household, into a sickroom, into the local church, into the church at large, out into the pagan world.

Every act of intercession is like the opening of a tap whose hidden conduits run back to the divine reservoir; like the throwing of a master switch that floods the immediate, local situation with all the power reserves of God—just because one Christian soul, conscious of its emptiness and need, opens its life Godwards, and finds all the fullness of Christ is at his call.

23

Overflowing on the Street
Colossians 4:5, 6

In *Hand Gathered Fruit* Edward Last tells of writing to two hundred young men who *in one year* had committed their lives to Christ during personal conversations with him on the streets of Glasgow. In nine and a half years, seven hundred and seventy-seven new members were added to his church, mainly by chain reactions originating in the daily, individualized testimony of this remarkable man. The book is full of the most moving evidence of the power of personal witness by one overflowing with the fullness of Christ.

So stimulated, memory recalls Annie Smith of the famous Tent Hall in Glasgow. On a tram car slowly threading its way through the

Saturday evening crowd in Argyle Street, she found herself seated
beside a drunken man in maudlin state. With her tremendous earnestness, wit, and forthrightness she set about leading him to Christ, and
before the journey was through was kneeling with him in prayer, in
a silent car which the driver moved at a snail's pace lest the intense
struggle for a soul should be disturbed.

Three or four poor women held godly talk together as they sat at
a door in the sunshine. One who was himself something of a brisk
talker on religion drew near and listened, but he soon found their
talk was above him. "They moved in a world of which he knew
nothing; they spoke of a holy discontent with themselves, and of a
new birth from above; they told how God had visited their souls with
His love in the Lord Jesus, and with what words and promises they
had been refreshed, comforted and strengthened; they 'spake as if
joy did make them speak,' with such 'pleasantness of scripture language, and with such appearance of grace in all they said' that they
seemed to him to have found a new world to which he was altogether
a stranger"—so John Brown describes a stage in the conversion experience of the great John Bunyan. Perhaps that explains why so
great a part of Bunyan's account of the journey from the City of
Destruction to the Celestial City consists of wayside conversations.

Many centuries before, Israel had been charged to keep faithfully
the words of God, "talking of them . . . by the way" (Deuteronomy
11:19 RSV). Philip, falling in with the eunuch on his journey home-
wards from the festival at Jerusalem, sitting as a hitchhiker in the
Ethiopian's sumptuous chariot and leading him to Christ, is in the
same tradition. But greatest of all the occasional roadside conversations that have marked turning points in religious history, occurred
on the road to Emmaus: two walked home through the evening, sad
at heart—and Jesus Himself drew near, and walked, and talked, with
transforming effect.

The full heart cannot help overflowing—anywhere. The man with
a faith to tell, a joy to share, will not be able to confine his overflowing
spirit to church, or home, or his work circle, or his private devotion.
There remains the neighborhood, the wider circle of friends, acquain-
tances, casual encounters. Almost every life has numberless personal
contacts, routine or accidental—ten a day, seventy a week, thirty-six
hundred a year! Its outer circumference touches the outer circumference of countless other lives, with varying degrees of impact: but

every separate intersection becomes a channel of outflow, a contact point at which the Christ-filled life discharges something of its power into other lives.

For the Christ-filled life must overflow. On the street, in the office, the shop, the schoolroom, among friends and colleagues and correspondents, in games circles, cultural assemblies, professional coteries, chance meetings with "those that are without," the quality of our lives is continually revealed—for good or ill. When life is filled with Christ, steadfast witness is not so much a duty as an inevitable consequence. For the Christ-filled life is pervasive, contagious, self-propagating, and cannot be hid. Nevertheless, Paul offers simple counsel intended to make our daily outside witness more effective.

Be willing to witness, says Paul, much as Jesus said "Let your light shine" and remarked the stupidity of lighting a candle only to conceal it beneath a vessel. The counsel seems superfluous, until one realizes how negative is the prevailing attitude of keen Christians toward the world around them.

The temptation of all ingroups, as Paul the Pharisee well understood, is to withdraw into their own circle of like-minded people. The righteous are so often self-righteous, so careful to keep themselves unspotted from the world that they fail to minister to the world. The saved are sometimes so unsure of their own safety that they avoid all contact with sinners they should win for Christ. Sometimes we imagine we have discharged all duty to society when we have warned, and condemned, though never once have we been ready to witness, to explain, to invite, to sympathize, to reconcile, to persuade.

Such negative reaction is selfish, immature, profitless—but above all, un-Christlike. For He was Friend of sinners. As a physician goes out toward the sick, as the shepherd goes after the sheep, as the grieving housewife hunts the lost coin, as the true friend pursues the wayward and the servant addresses himself to the appointed task— each a gospel metaphor describing Jesus—so the Christian following His example does not turn his back upon the needy, sick, lost, wayward, helpless world, or any member of it. He is more than willing, he is *eager* to tell of his Saviour and share the fullness of the riches of Christ with all who will receive.

Be awake, Paul adds, awake to the opportunities, perhaps again remembering a word of Jesus about the servant whom his master shall find not slumbering, but wakeful for his lord's return and review of his work. Paul's suggestion for making the most of the time is to buy up every opening and catch every fleeting bargain. Someone has suggested his words really mean "corner the market" so as to keep out all other bidders for men's souls.

That, at any rate, is the implication of Paul's similar counsel to the Ephesians: ". . . making the most of the time, because the days are evil" (Ephesians 5:16 RSV). The peril in which all men stand will not allow procrastination. But neither can we ourselves afford to miss opportunities of serving the Master: we live all our days on borrowed time, and only the alert soul wins from each fleeting hour its due return of worthwhile work attempted.

"Never pray for opportunities," a faithful mentor once advised. "Pray for grace to take the opportunities God has given—you will find them quite enough!" Those most experienced, and most used, in daily personal testimony for Christ are usually those who deeply deplore the openings missed, the occasions when they were unready. Frances Ridley Havergal entertained village girls at her country home, eager to help and befriend them. Years later, she sat beside a dying woman who revealed that she had been one of those girls frequenting the Havergal home. "I often wished in those days," the sick woman said, "that you would speak to me about my soul. I lingered at the gate hoping you would. Afterwards, someone else led me to the Saviour—but I ought to have been yours, Miss Frances, I ought to have been yours."

Yet to be willing, and awake, may make us overeager, religious bores rather than bearers of salvation. *Be wise,* says Paul again. Sometimes he asks for honesty and peaceableness toward them that are without: but he pleads for wisdom, and intelligence, three times. As someone has said, Paul advises walking in wisdom—he abhors walking in craftiness. There is certainly a difference.

Wisdom in approaching others for Christ involves insight, to know the right word; sympathy, to know the right way; patience, to discern the right time. To "know how you ought to answer every one" demands that you address yourself to the single person where he is, bringing the fullness of Christ to bear upon every separate circumstance in every individual situation. Generalities are useless, and often cruel: the flippant offer of a text can be the mean substitute for genuine attempts to understand.

When Peter counsels us to be ready with an answer for any who ask us to explain our hope, he too urges that we shall do so "with gentleness and reverence." "He that winneth souls is wise"—he has to be: more positive harm is done by crassly incompetent and aggressive evangelism than by any other form of Christian blundering. Yet it is not cleverness, or training, that confers the necessary wit, but humble dependence upon God, true concern for people, and a simple love for Christ. These three will ensure against the worst mistakes, and experience and the guidance of the Holy Spirit will teach us the rest.

Finally, and unexpectedly, Paul says, *Be winsome.* "Be pleasant, gracious," he advises, talking with grace as well as about grace. Be nice to talk to, able to listen, agreeable, charming, courteous in reply, interesting because you are interested, and easy to confide in because you inspire confidence.

Who can measure the need of that particular appeal! The belligerently religious are the faith's worst foes; they break the bruised reed and quench the smoking flax of faith; they ridicule young inquirers' questions, roughly override sincere and searching doubts, criticize mistakes and failures so harshly that sad hearts do not want to try again. Not so the Master. When He spoke, men wondered at the gracious words that fell from His lips; His authority and forthrightness and fearlessness and truth were all clothed with a gentleness and concern that made the common people hear Him gladly. It will often be that those who come to us for counsel go away again still unbelieving and unwilling; but they should *never* go away sorry that they ever came.

Paul adds to winsomeness of speech the quality of piquancy, point, and pungency—what the Greeks called "salty speech," conversation that has flavor, interest, wit, and memorable meaning. This does surprise us, but there is no reason at all why the Christian should be dull or undiscriminating. The man in earnest about winning others, and full of his subject, Christ, will find the bright ideas come, the bright words flow, the right way to put things given him by the Spirit, if only he is setting out to be genuinely interesting and to persuade. But he who is merely saying his piece, delivering his own conscience, airing his religious opinions, and showing where he stands, will bore the angels.

If any man's life be full of Christ it will overflow: but willingness, wakefulness, wisdom, and winsomeness will ensure that it overflows to some purpose.

"I early learned," says John Burroughs the American naturalist, quoted by Edward Last, "that from almost any stream in a trout country the true angler could take a trout, and that the great secret was this: that whatever bait you used . . . one thing you must always put upon your hook, namely your heart. With such a bait . . . the born angler . . . used his hook so coyly and tenderly, he approached the fish with such address and insinuation . . . if they were not eager, he humored them; if they were playful and coquettish, he would suit his mood to theirs; if they were frank and sincere, he met them halfway. Patient and considerate . . . how nicely he would measure the distance, how dexterously he would drop the line in exactly the right spot . . . ."

All that—*for trout!* How much more skillful and devoted must be fishers of men, whose purpose is not to catch or exploit, or proudly display as conquests, but to share with others the fullness of Christ who is everything to us.

24

Overflowing in Christian Fellowship
COLOSSIANS 4:7-11

It is one of the marks of Paul's quick, fertile, rich mind that in the midst of careful exposition or strong argument he sometimes slips in unpremeditated comments which are intriguing, and often revealing. How much of his inner heart is compressed in the sudden phrase, after the name of God—"whose I am, and whom I serve" (Acts 27:23). And in the moving words added to the name of Christ— "who loved me, and gave himself for me" (Galatians 2:20). Of another kind, revealing sadness and disappointment, is the aside in this passage: Aristarchus, Mark, and Jesus called Justus—"These are the only men of the circumcision among my fellow workers for the kingdom of God, and they have been a comfort to me" (RSV).

There is no doubt that is what Paul wrote, despite some blundering translations, and there is no mistaking the poignancy of the remark.

It is not only that Paul, a patriotic Jew to the end, would have valued the support and approval of his fellow Jews in the common hope of the Messiah's kingdom. It is not only that he recoiled with pain from misunderstanding of his message and misrepresentation of his motives. Deeper still, in the fewness of his Jewish friends lay something wholly alien to Paul's nature.

For Paul was essentially a teamworker. The large number of his named colleagues is often remarked, and most of them were devoted to his leadership. Repeatedly, he pleads that others will remember him in prayer. On one occasion he would not visit a church lest he be personally rejected and friendship be finally broken; meanwhile he was too distressed and anxious even to preach the gospel. At the end of his life, the sense of loneliness adds sharply to his pain: "Only Luke is with me" (2 Timothy 4:11), and again ". . . no man stood with me" (2 Timothy 4:16). Paul was a companionable man, and T. R. Glover well notes that he seems to have been uneasy when left alone.

To such men, the fellowship of kindred minds is essential. Division from others over truth and principle may have to be faced and accepted, but only as a last resort and with intense regret. Whenever possible, despite distances and the difficulties of correspondence, Paul would keep in touch, send news, exchange greetings, arrange visits, send representatives when he could not travel himself. Always names are remembered, and sickness, or other circumstances, recalled, affection is voiced, and faithful prayer assured—because in Paul a naturally sociable and outreaching temperament had been confirmed by the experience of Christian fellowship.

So in writing to Colossae, Paul charges the bearers of the letter, Tychicus and Onesimus, to tell all about his affairs. "I have sent him to you for this very purpose," he says, "that you may know how we are and that he may encourage your hearts, And with him Onesimus . . . . They will tell you of everything that has taken place here" (RSV). To Paul, it was worth any effort to preserve and to strengthen the links that bound Christians across the Roman Empire.

That is why his letters usually begin and end with other names beside his own. Sometimes the individual personalities are uppermost in his mind, sometimes their work; in this epilogue to the Colossian letter, both are emphasized. Confining attention for the present to the men themselves, we cannot miss the care with which each is loyally commended and individually valued. Each is remembered clearly:

Timothy beside Paul, Aristarchus sharing imprisonment, Tychicus on his journey, Epaphras at his prayers, others in their assemblies at Colossae, Hierapolis, and Laodicea. To move among the Pauline circle, even at this distance of time, is to feel the variety, the depth, and the strenuousness, of that Christian fellowship which Paul so highly values.

For example, we note the humble Tychicus beside the exceptionally gifted Luke. Tychicus is usually designated "humble" but it is an inference rather from absence of information than from positive knowledge. A trusted personal assistant, sometimes a delegate, usually a messenger and bearer of letters, Tychicus was a man to be sent here, or left there, or appointed elsewhere, as best served the cause. Paul's trust in him for such lowly tasks is his chief claim to remembrance.

In sharpest contrast stands Luke, a master of Greek style, a poet, some say a painter—he can certainly paint with words—a physician, too, and a steadfast friend. Traveling with Paul, and keeping notes of important occasions, Luke gives us the invaluable first account of the growing church. Even more important, Luke gave us "the most beautiful book in the world," as the historian Renan called it, the Gospel of Jesus the Jewish Saviour as seen through gentile eyes. When Paul calls him "the dear friend," something of personal gratitude for medical care in days of suffering and need probably lends warmth to the words.

Quite different again appears Aristarchus, "on every mention of whom we wish we knew more." Calling him "fellow prisoner," Paul seems unlikely to mean simply "captured by Christ"—which could be said of every Christian. More probably, he means that just as in the riot at Ephesus, on the journey from Corinth amid the plotting of the Jews, and on the fateful journey to Rome, so now in his imprisonment, the loyal Aristarchus is at Paul's side, imprisoned either for his own witness or as Paul's attendant. "Clearly," says William Barclay, Aristarchus was "a good man to have about you in a tight corner." Few could wish greater commendation than that.

But of "Jesus called Justus," who is "made immortal in three words" as Maclaren said, we know nothing more. If the epithet means the same as when applied to James, presumably this Christian Jesus was honored as a strict and loyal Jew; though it could of course indicate uprightness, rather than strictness.

Here is a varied quartet of Christian friends, different as could be, but each valued. No doubt Paul would say of these also, "they have been a comfort to me": the expression is said to be a medical one—"they have been a cordial to refresh my spirit."

The strenuousness of that apostolic fellowship is exhibited in the way it holds on resolutely to those about whose previous story there were elements that might easily have excluded them. This is obviously true of Onesimus, but also of Mark, and possibly of Demas.

Onesimus had offended deeply, by disloyalty and disobedience toward his master, Philemon, a member of one of the local churches; he had aggravated that offense by theft of his master's property; and he had broken all the rules that governed his place in society by fleeing from his master's control, placing his very life in danger. On all counts, he was a criminal.

It is true that he had since been converted to Christ, and he is being sent back to his master and to his home district as now faithful, beloved, and a brother. But his offenses were serious, and all Philemon's equals would urge that leniency was dangerous. Even Christian slaves might draw perilous conclusions from Onesimus's example. Paul refrains from comment here, though in his private note to Philemon he says much. For the church, Paul leaves Tychicus and Onesimus to tell the story as it should be told, face-to-face; but he delicately assumes, in his threefold tribute, that the church will welcome Onesimus as a brother.

The phrase "who is one of yourselves" can hardly be intended to inform the Colossians that Onesimus is from one of their own church families. It must surely be the one hint in this letter of what Paul expects—that the Christian fellowship at Colossae will be generous enough, forgiving enough, and firm enough to their principles, to welcome Onesimus henceforth as "one of themselves," for such he now is.

It is strange that Colossae should show any reluctance to welcome Mark; we know of no convincing reason. Yet Paul deliberately recalls some instructions that someone has already given concerning this, and they are now reinforced by the direct appeal, "if he comes to you, receive him." Whether the old disappointment over Mark's defection from the first missionary journey twelve years before had been reported at Colossae; or whether his close connection with Peter made him suspect as one of the Judaizing party who so often opposed Paul, we cannot say; neither explanation seems plausible.

Whatever the suspicion, or coolness, in which Mark stood at Colossae, Paul affirms the claims of Christian fellowship in order to bring it to an end. "Receive him" is a brief instruction, almost per-emptory, and sufficient: "Let there be an end to this nonsense!" Estrangements, for any cause, must not be allowed to last. One fas-cinating footnote to these greetings from Mark and Luke arises from their presence together in the company of Paul: two gospel writers, and the apostle of the Gentiles—what conversations that conjures up!

Of Demas nothing at all is said, except that he joins Luke in sending greeting. That he may have been writing the letter at Paul's dictation scarcely explains this; Paul's "secretaries" are sometimes mentioned with affection. That a Demas is mentioned again with Mark and Luke in the Second Letter to Timothy suggests this is the man who there has deserted Paul, being "in love with this present world." Was there something about Demas's character already evident to Paul, which made him withhold comment or commendation, while not excluding him from the exchange of greetings? Christian fellow-ship must ever stretch its loving concern over the erring as long as opportunity remains. The faithless may excommunicate themselves: true Christian friendship never withdraws its compassion or its prayers.

Thus against actual wrong, suspected wrong, and threatened wrong, the bonds of Christian love strain to hold Christians together. Like Christ's own love, it will not willingly let men go. Throughout this letter Paul has emphasized the unity of Christians against the divisive-ness of the false teaching infiltrating Colossae. Equally, he has empha-sized that Christ is the Reconciler of all things, in every realm, the Head and center of that unity which God purposes to restore to His creation. One of the great affirmations of the epistle is that in Christ there cannot be racial divisions, ritual divisions, cultural or social divisions, because Christ is all, and in all. And he has shown how the fullness of life in Christ overflows in social ways in church, home, and community.

It is not surprising then that Paul should see in the Christian comradeship that reached from the Colossian valley to people his prison with friends, an indispensable part of the work of Christ, and a characteristic fruit of the gospel. The fullness of Christ must over-flow in the fellowship of saints.

But with the letter to the Ephesians in our hands, we can discern another reason why an epistle on the fullness of Christ should end with an emphasis on Christian fellowship. For we learn that in Paul's view the fullness of Christ is too great, too rich, too inexhaustible, for individual comprehension. None of us possesses the whole Christ: but only just so much as our partial, limited, inhibited apprehension can grasp. The fullness of Christ is embodied in all, not in each. Only "with all the saints" can the individual comprehend "what is the breadth and length and height and depth," and only "with all the saints" can he know the love which surpasses knowledge, so being "filled with all the fullness of God."

Any breach of fellowship, therefore, involves impoverishment for both sides in our understanding of Christ. Separated from our brethren, we are in that degree farther from the total Christ, who is present only in the total experience of the whole fellowship. Only as we work and worship, witness and live within the bonds of that fellowship can we know the fullness of Him that filleth all in all.

> Rich by my brethren's poverty?
> Such wealth were worthless! I am blest
> Only in what they share with me,
> In what I share with all the rest.

25

Overflowing in Christian Service
COLOSSIANS 4:12-17

As Paul closes this rich and forceful exposition of the fullness of Christ, his emphasis falls upon the deep mutual fellowship between Christians, in which the individual's experience of that fullness finds expression, and is enhanced, in the shared experience of the community. In part, Paul is thinking of the varied personalities that make up the circle of that fellowship, linking him with otherwise unknown Colossae. But equally, he thinks of the varied service of the kingdom in which these different personalities share.

For the bonds of Christian comradeship comprise not only the joint inheritance of a great faith and the sharing together of a transforming experience but the common service of an exhilarating cause. If the truth be told, sometimes we find in working together an easier path to Christian understanding and cooperation than in discussion, or worship, or even in prayer. But what an infinitely varied service the kingdom demands of its subjects! There is room in the work of Christ for all types of worker, for people of ten talents, or five, or one—and it is a basic assumption of the gospel that there is no one who lacks talent entirely. Christ allows us to think no man worthless, and no life useless if it be surrendered to Him.

In this closing passage of Colossians, Paul himself represents the *apostles,* men of a special commission from the Lord Himself; and of a special qualification, being eyewitnesses of the risen Christ. Such formed the natural leaders, the inherent authorities of the infant church, the source of continued inspiration, and the channels of special powers granted by the Spirit.

For the same reasons, the apostles were also distinguished as major targets for the enemies of the church. As Paul ironically claims: ". . . I think that God has exhibited us apostles as last of all, like men sentenced to death" (1 Corinthians 4:9 rsv)—he is thinking, evidently, of the gladiatorial shows in the arena—"because we have become a spectacle to the world, to angels, and to men . . . . we have become, and are now, as the refuse of the world, the offscouring of all things" (1 Corinthians 4:9, 13 rsv). Any who in our day aspire to, or claim, apostleship do well to remember its condition—the infilling of the Spirit; and its cost, trying to imagine what apostolic "success" felt like on the inside.

Beside the apostles were their *helpers,* personal assistants like Tychicus and Mark here, Timothy and Silas mentioned elsewhere, and many others. Someone always has to arrange the details, the food, clothing, hospitality, times, dates, advertising, and travel. If the work is to be unhindered, and the Lord's gifts are not to be squandered, the planning had better be efficiently executed. Many large visions and fine enterprises have come to nothing because no one posted the letters, booked the halls, got the printing done, and dusted the church! The cause of Christ owes an immense debt to the countless unseen helpers without whom leaders in the public eye would be helpless—and useless.

Among the fellow servants of Paul was Luke, the dear physician, splendid representative of a magnificent host who have followed, down the centuries, in his steps. For many centuries, and increasingly in recent years, the whole field of medical care, research, alleviation, and preventive planning, of specialized attention to the old, the child, the handicapped, the mentally deranged, the educationally subnormal, has been appreciated as a sphere of Christian ministry at least as important as the ministry of the spoken gospel.

For that assessment, the very highest authority is at hand. From the miracle ministry of Jesus, followed by the healings practised in the apostolic church, and flowing from the active compassion native to Christian love, sounds the call that created the medical missions, the countless relief societies and medical charities, the village dispensaries, the leper colonies and asylums for the insane, the great teaching and research hospitals, and the vast laboratories. That call has been answered wonderfully in the quiet dedication, the self-sacrifice, the arduous application to study, the brilliance and imagination of innumerable scientists, specialists, doctors, nurses, opticians, dentists, and experts of many kinds.

We conceive Christ's service much too narrowly if we think only of ability to speak or pray in public, or to organize church work. As Christ is Saviour of the whole man, so Christian service washes the feet of the needy, suffering world with the same devotion to Christ that seeks the lost soul. "Inasmuch as you did it to one of the least of these . . . you did it unto me" is instruction, call, and inspiration enough.

But Luke, standing here beside Mark, recalls yet another sphere of Christian ministry—*education*. For these two were writers—as indeed Paul himself was. Without Mark's gospel, we would have lost probably the most precious book in the world, the earliest, eyewitness account of the Master, so vivid, so dramatic, so unstudied and forceful. Without Luke's supplement we should have lost some of the most precious of His sayings and parables, and one of the tenderest portraits of Jesus ever penned. Without Paul's correspondence, not only our New Testament but our spiritual experience would be immeasurably poorer.

Who shall assess what has been accomplished for Christ's cause by skilled and faithful writers, scholars, teachers, poets, hymnists, through whom the faith of the church has been clarified and perpetuated, the experience of the church has been bequeathed in permanent form to subsequent generations, and the vision of the church has been so often broadened or rekindled? There is a significant corner in church history for the great books that have changed men's minds, redeemed an age, met a challenge, reopened fruitfully forgotten questions, or brought light and warmth to persistent problems. With the widening literacy of the world, the call to serve Christ by writing and by education of all kinds is increasingly insistent. In a print-hungry world, the pen may well be mightier than the pulpit.

Epaphras, too, stands in Paul's closing paragraph, as he stood in the opening chapter, glowing with Paul's praise. His identification with his people, and his dedication to their welfare, shown in a pastor's unremitting labor in all schemes and routines that promote the *ministry* of his church, and in a pastor's unremitting intercession for the members and the work, show yet another form of Christian service demanded in every age.

Even in these days of mass communication and high-pressure publicizing, even of the gospel itself, a key position in the work of Christ undoubtedly still belongs to the local minister—preacher, pastor, evangelist, counselor. Whatever changes may affect the church, the characteristics of her life, as Luke describes them, will remain: she will continue in the apostles' teaching and fellowship, in breaking of bread, and in prayers. And wherever these abide, the local leader will be needed, and will emerge, to mediate that teaching, to be a focus of that fellowship, to conduct that memorial worship, and foster that life of prayer. The call to the pastoral office remains among the most challenging of all calls to serve Christ, even as its demands upon intellect, maturity, patience, and persistence, continually increase.

This is because, amid all changes, the *local fellowship* must remain the growing point of Christianity. This is the threshold where the new convert makes contact with the universal church of all ages; here, as Peter T. Forsyth taught, the universal church, the Body of Christ, "emerges in a given place." Paul valued highly these little, localized Christian assemblies, at Colossae, Hierapolis, Laodicea, and elsewhere, as the indispensable units that together comprised the church of Christ.

That the church met "in the house of Nympha" (RSV) reminds us that as yet she possessed no places of worship, but depended upon the hospitality of members whose homes could become the centers of assembly and of fellowship. Here is another prized avenue of Christian service: the *hospitality* that in every age has provided a nursery for young converts, refuge for the persecuted, shelter for the homeless, retreat for the broken, the addict, the lost, and the meeting place for Bible study and prayer when the church has been pilgrim and stranger in the earth. The Christian home has ever been our faith's most potent investment: so many times through history, the open door of Christian hospitality has entertained angels unaware.

Finally, and almost as an afterthought, Paul sent a special word to a young servant of the kingdom, apparently just beginning his work for Christ. Archippus, son of Philemon and Apphia, prominent members of one of the Lycus Valley churches, had evidently been appointed by the Colossian church to some position of leadership. From the tone of Paul's message, resembling that of the pastoral epistles, it seems he was both young and in need of strengthening: ". . . say to Archippus, take heed to the ministry which thou hast received in the Lord, that thou fulfil it."

It is very odd that Paul should send counsel to the minister of one of these churches through its members. Paul urges the church to encourage him, now that it has appointed him; to see that no patronizing overfamiliarity, no criticism, no failure in loyalty or respect shall hinder his fulfillment of his calling. The church that makes a man a minister has so very large a responsibility in the making, or unmaking, of his ministry.

At the same time, Archippus is reminded that though the call to ministry has come through his friends and fellow deacons and members, still the call is from the Lord—not a plan thought up by Mom and Dad and a few companions in the church. The human arrangement is but the channel of a divine commission that makes him the Lord's servant, and not man's.

Nor can we miss the lingering echo of the central theme of Paul's letter in the phrase "Fill to the full your ministry." That means more than "make the most of it": Paul reminds the young minister once again that Christ is our fullness, and He must be allowed to fill our ministry, overflowing through us to those whom God has given us. Every young minister is tempted to be somewhat "full of himself," and not young ministers only. But at heart we all know that only the fullness of Christ can match our ministry to our people's need.

Paul was a realist. He has discoursed on high themes: the fullness of deity indwelling Christ; Christ as agent and sustainer, focus and goal of all creation; the fullness of "all the good that is ours in Christ" pouring into each believer who holds fast by Him; the overflow of that fullness into church worship, into Christian homelife, through the Christian at work and in prayer, into the Christian's neighborhood, and through the Christian fellowship. Now at the close, he bids us realize that the fullness of Christ pours onward, outward into the world, and downward through the course of history, as in innumerable places, often small and obscure, the work of Christ is patiently done by groups of faithful souls, servants of the kingdom, each filled with the fullness of Christ.

When we come down to it, this is the truth of the matter. Paul's great concept of the fullness of Christ and the consequent fullness of Christian living finds effective expression, and bears enduring fruit, in the little house-churches and local personal ministries that from Paul's time until ours make up the story of Christ's kingdom. Our place may be small, our talent limited, our results few, but the call is not to succeed but to serve; "we preach not ourselves, but Christ Jesus the Lord"; our answer to the world's deep hunger and thirst is not anything we can say or do—but the fullness of Him that filleth all in all.

Our generation lives in a spiritual vacuum, and the heart of our world is empty. Who then will go, will serve, will tell—of Him in whom all fullness dwells?

26

The Fullness and the Fetters
COLOSSIANS 4:18

To suspect Paul of deliberately contriving a highly dramatic ending to his letter, after the manner of some artist of the theater, would be stupid. He was far too earnest a writer and pastor to concern himself with artificial effects. Yet had he sought long for a striking and memorable close, an exit line that would clinch the play, he could have found no better than the simple: "I Paul write this greeting with my own hand. Remember my fetters" (RSV).

The great difficulty about such a theme as has occupied Colossians is that most of us assent to it without believing it. The fullness of Christ is part of our faith, certainly. He is the divine Son, the ever-living Lord, in whom the fullness of the Godhead dwells. The fullness of Christian life, too, is our hope and goal—one day. Meanwhile, we have work to do, sins to fight, handicaps of all kinds to overcome,

difficulties to resolve, wasted opportunities to regret, limited understanding, limited resources, and very limited faith. The glorious faith
of the gospel, the splendid ideal of the Christ-filled life, coexist in
thought with doubts, problems, disappointments, and failures. They
never coincide in personal experience.

To that misgiving, Paul's closing words provide the perfect answer.
For here are two reminders of Paul's own unhappy position as he
writes. One is a hint, a probability; the other a clear fact. Together,
they set the whole message of the letter in eloquent paradox, and bring
the apostle with his soaring affirmations and searching ideals very
close indeed alongside ourselves.

The Fetters That Accompany the Fullness

The hint, or probability, about Paul's unhappy situation is in the
words "I Paul write this greeting with my own hand." Paul often
dictated his letters; at the end of Romans we are told that Tertius did
the actual writing, and in other epistles we are plainly informed when
Paul took the pen in hand to make his signature. But often the reason
is given: in the letter to Philemon, it is because a promise to pay
should be in the debtor's own handwriting; in the second letter to
Thessalonica it is because the church has been disturbed by forged
letters "purporting to be from" Paul. His signature is expressly declared to be "the mark in every letter of mine." At the end of First
Corinthians the signature may be to avoid accusations in that divided
church that some one party is misrepresenting Paul's counsel.

But why sign Colossians? And why is the salutation and benedic-
tion so very brief—almost curt? Comparison with the letter to the
Galatians suggests a reason why Paul dictated at all. For there, Paul
remarks playfully the large, "child's" letters which he uses when he
tries to write; and earlier, recalling that he had preached in Galatia
at the first beset by some "bodily ailment," he says, ". . . you would
have plucked out your eyes and given them to me" (Galatians 4:15
RSV). Was Paul subject to some ophthalmic trouble which made writing painful, slow, and clumsy, so that he used the pen only when
occasion demanded?

This cannot be proved. But there is no possible doubt that Paul
struggled constantly against some bodily infirmity, that occasionally
made others report of him contemptuously, "his bodily presence is
weak," and which made Paul himself beg God repeatedly that the

thorn might be removed from his flesh. The presence with him so often of Luke the physician confirms this picture of a man driving himself constantly to the limit of his strength, and needing often the ministrations of one skilled to restore his exhausted powers. "The outward man is perishing," Paul confesses, and elsewhere he admits to weariness often, affliction, hardship, calamity. Paul was no invalid, but it seems he could have been one, but for that immense and restless energy, that passionate love for Christ, which fired his weakened frame. An infirm and afflicted man—and the fullness of Christ!

The second reminder in Paul's so brief salutation is explicit enough: "Remember my fetters." As he writes to Colossae, Paul is in prison, apparently in chains. Either to appeal for prayer on his behalf, or to reinforce his counsel by proving his own zeal for the truth and care for the churches, Paul vividly reminds us, before the letter closes, of the sad circumstances from which it issued. That wide-ranging life has narrowed down to a small prison cell; that restless spirit and never satisfied energy is forcibly held in check, shackled in uselessness; those tireless feet can now pace only the length of a single room, and the gaze that ever dreamed beyond the distant horizon is now fixed on an opposite wall.

That no power on earth could really confine that soaring intellect and mighty heart, only intensified the repression and constraint of prison life and enforced inactivity. Paul in prison, an infirm and afflicted man—and the fullness of Christ!

It is, then, out of a situation of affliction, confinement, and frustration that Paul writes with enthusiasm of the overflowing fullness to be found in Christ. The letter to the Colossians reveals the same kind of paradox that makes the letter to Philippi so striking. Philippians is the epistle of imprisonment and joy, of peril and praise; it corresponds very remarkably to Paul's experience at Philippi—darkness, pain, an inner cell, and danger, with songs in the night. Colossians is the epistle of fetters and fullness, of limitation of circumstances and unlimited resources of power and joy, of the apostle's body shut fast in a cell, while his mind and spirit range through the height and depth of Christian faith and experience.

This is the first answer to the misgiving that the teaching of the epistle is too remote, its aspiration too high, for ordinary Christians, limited, handicapped, beset with problems and imperfections: the letter was born in trouble in order to show that the fullness of Christ is available for all—however circumscribed their circumstances, however difficult their way. "In Him dwells the fullness"—not in us; as we lay hold of Him the fullness floods our lives, whatever the fetters or the fears might be. The Christ-filled life is revealed, not in the absence of difficulties, but in triumph over them.

But Paul goes further.

The Fullness That Cannot Be Fettered

The mere existence of the letter to Colossae illustrates this: first Epaphras, then Colossae, and eventually all Christendom have felt the impact of four short chapters crammed with the large thought and immeasurable confidence of Paul. Not all the might of Rome could effectively confine him to a prison cell, nor Christianity to a few small and scattered communities; the fullness of Christ in Paul has overflowed through centuries of Christian history and to the edges of the world.

But Paul's own thought presents this truth more dramatically. He has insisted that the fullness dwells in Christ, *never in us*. We are but vehicles, channels, of a grace and wisdom and power not our own. Our sickness, imprisonment, frustration, even our failure, cannot diminish the sufficiency of Christ. We are conductors—the power is His: ". . . we have this treasure in earthen vessels, that the excellency of the power may be of God, and not of us" (2 Corinthians 4:7).

For Paul this is no reverent acknowledgement of dependence: it is a fact of experience. To know the fullness of Christ in himself, and to mediate that fullness into the world, a man needs not to be clever or successful, talented or highly trained, fortunate in circumstances or even fit in health. Paul even suggests that the more he relies upon such fortuitous advantages, the less will be his experience of Christ's power.

". . . when I am weak, then am I strong" (2 Corinthians 12:10)— that is Paul's summary of his own discovery, covering both his infirmity and his physical peril at Ephesus. He implies that he had thought otherwise, for he prayed often to be set free, given a better chance, the liberty to work without handicap or hindrance. But the prayer had been denied. In effect, the Lord said: "For yourself, my grace is sufficient for you; as for the work, my strength is made perfect in your weakness." Paul makes the splendid response, "Most gladly therefore will I rather glory in my infirmities, that the power of

Christ may rest upon me. I am content with weakness, insults, hardships, persecutions and calamities, for when I am weak, then am I strong."

So Paul writes to Corinth, but that is precisely the paradox of Colossians. Writing out of identical circumstances, Paul expounds the richness, the inexhaustible wisdom, the unquenchable gratitude and hope, the invincible power and grace of the life filled with the divine Christ. The circumstances are irrelevant to the infilling, though they will determine just how the fullness finds expression. The one thing that no prison, or handicap, or frustrating lack of cleverness or training, or ill health, or want of money, or any similar hindrance can do, is to fetter the Christ who dwells within us, our hope of glory.

The church discovered this as she surveyed her membership and felt within her the throb of a divine energy: "You see your calling, brethren: not many wise, according to worldly standards, not many powerful, or of noble birth; but God chose what is foolish in the world to shame the wise, God chose what is weak in the world to shame the strong, God chose what is low and despised in the world, even things that are not, to bring to nothing things that are" (*see* 1 Corinthians 1:26). The fullness could not be fettered.

Rome discovered this, as she surveyed her attempts to break the church and eliminate the faith, for the more she persecuted, the more Christianity prospered. Rome could not bend the church to her will, nor frighten her into silence, nor stem the outflow of that strong tide of spiritual life and power by which she lived. Rome in the end could only succumb, and declare herself Christian. The fullness could not be fettered.

And wonderingly, the Christians discovered it too. An unbreakable courage, an unflinching loyalty to Christ, a resilience and buoyancy of spirit, an inner resource of endurance and joy were manifest in ordinary, humble people, that surprised each other and astonished themselves. In the few references to martyrdom within the New Testament, and increasingly in the second century, one feels this curious double reaction to persecution: heroism is expected of ordinary Christians—and when it is shown, all the honor and courage and grace to suffer nobly and without bitterness are ascribed to the grace of Christ, through whose strengthening they could do all things, and through whose love they became more than conquerors.

This is the second answer to the misgiving that the teaching of this epistle is too remote, its aspiration too high, for limited, handicapped, imperfect Christians. Fetters may accompany the fullness—but the fullness cannot be fettered. This is the heart of the message of Colossians. "In Christ dwells all the fullness of the Godhead, bodily, and you are filled full in Him"; that fullness of Christian living admits no barriers, hindrances, checks or fetters, save only this: that we do not let Him fill us with His fullness. Only our refusal can fetter His fullness—refusal to believe it possible, refusal to make room for Him, refusal to lay hold of all He offers us. "In Him dwells all the fullness" —only the blind and foolish would turn empty away.

O Lord of infinite mercy and plenteous redemption,
Giver of all immeasurable things,
Source of life abundant, love eternal, hope beyond all calculation,
Laying within human reach pearls of great price, riches unsearchable,
    and harvest a hundredfold,
Lord of the full cup, the brimming river, the well too deep to draw, the
    perpetual spring within the soul,
Thyself the unutterable gift, of whose fullness have all we received,
Have pity on our poverty!

Forgive the emptiness of lives content to ask without expecting to receive;
Forgive the hollowness of thought concealed by clever words;
Forgive the barrenness of hearts no longer moved, or movable;
Forgive the weak infirmity of wills no longer brave, or resolute.
Forgive the want of vision, faith, and eagerness, that beggars all our life
    to bankruptcy; the counterfeit affluence, whose greater barns can
    scarce contain our folly and leave our very souls in debt.

Remind us, O God, that all things are ours as we are Christ's; that in
    Him dwells all the fullness, and we are full in Him;
Let our impoverished souls delight again in fatness, and overflow not
    only in compassion but with plenitude.

Enable us afresh to say, with truth, "Such as I have, give I unto thee
    . . ." and with overflowing hearts and hands to obey that word—
"Give ye them to eat"
                              for the world's sake, and for ours,
                              but in the Name of Him that filleth all in all.